ALL-TIME FAVORITE CARD GAMES

Publications International, Ltd.

David Galt is a game designer and consultant who has written extensively on games old and new. His articles have appeared in *Games* magazine, *The Playing Card,* and *Country Collectibles,* and he is also the author of *Card Games for One or Two.* His collection of over 5000 antique games and playing cards includes some of the first in America.

Cover illustration: Guy Wolek

Louis Weber, C.E.O.
Publications International, Ltd.
7373 North Cicero Avenue
Lincolnwood, Illinois 60646

Manufactured in U.S.A.

8 7 6 5 4 3 2 1

ISBN: 0-7853-2096-2

CONTENTS

IT'S IN THE CARDS

Can you keep a poker face and play it close to the vest? Well then, here's a not-so-well-kept secret: For the past 600 years, card games have been a great way for people of all ages to have fun!

Card games bring people together for amusement—that's why they've been around so long. Just listen to the words we use, and you'll hear plenty of everyday phrases that stem from the world of card playing.

A veteran Euchre player, for instance, knows the right time to "play a lone hand." "That goes double in spades" is often heard at Pinochle and Gin Rummy tables. Winners at Poker tend to have an "ace in the hole." In Solo, Setback, and Bezique, you must know when to "play your trump card."

Besides encouraging communication, cards teach us a lot. Children can learn about numbers through games such as Crazy Eights, Fan Tan,

and War. Casino, Cribbage, and Michigan are among the many games that show us the factor of luck. Spades and I Doubt It require sneaky tactics and a certain amount of guesswork.

Learn how to play these games and more! The following pages provide instructions for 29 of the most popular card games of all time. For each game, there are rules of play, a game objective, a suggested number of players, card requirements, and scoring rules. Also included

are tips to help you formulate a strategy, as well as variations for modifying each game. The rules

provided are merely guidelines; you may develop your own variations as well. The handy glossary should be useful for defining important terms.

So, if you're looking for exitement, look through this book. You're sure to find a card game to suit any occasion!

4

AUCTION PINOCHLE

Although Pinochle developed in Europe out of the popular game Bezique, immigrants to America probably invented Auction Pinochle. Its appeal was greatest a century ago, and many believe it to be the all-time-best three-handed card game.

Number of players: three (or four, with the dealer sitting out each deal)

Object: to score points in melds and in play

The cards: Use a 48-card Pinochle pack. You can put one together from two standard packs by dropping all deuces through 8s. The cards rank—from high to low—as follows: A-10-K-Q-J-9.

To play: Deal 15 cards to each player. By tradition, deal in bunches of three or one bunch of three followed by bunches of four. Deal three cards (not the last three) to a facedown widow, or kitty.

The bidding: Starting with the player at the dealer's left, each player bids or passes. The lowest bid is 250 points, and bids increase by ten points thereafter. Once you pass you can't reenter the bidding, but bidders can continue raising the auction. The auction is closed once two players have passed. The aim is to score at least as many points as you bid, by scoring for melds and winning tricks (see "Melds in Pinochle").

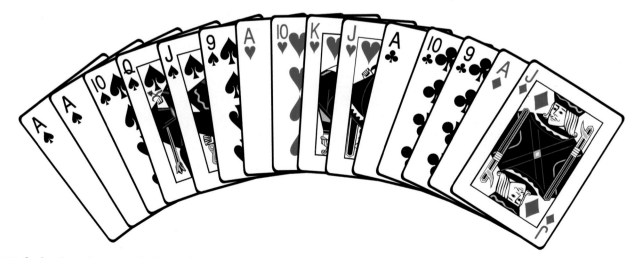

With this hand, a 300 bid is safe. You have 100 Aces to meld, plus pinochle (♠ Q-♥ J), and the dix of trump, worth 10. In play, your hand should take 150 points. You also have two flushes open, and if you get a lucky widow, you might have much more to meld. It's probably best not to risk a 400 bid on this type of hand.

The player who wins the bid becomes the bidder. If you are the bidder, turn the three widow cards faceup and add them to your hand. It may be clear at this point that your total of melds and cards you could take in play won't reach your bid. At this point, you have the option to concede, but if you concede, you lose the amount you bid. Otherwise, table your melds, including the cards from the widow, and announce a suit as trump. If you have already reached or exceeded the value of your bid, play ceases immediately, and you score the value of your game (see "Scoring").

Your two opponents will temporarily unite in their play against you. In order to reduce your hand back down to 15 cards, choose three unmelded cards to set aside, facedown, to add later to the tricks you win. Pick up your melds, and lead any card to the first trick.

The winner of each trick leads to the next. You must always follow suit, and if you cannot follow to a plain suit you must play a trump card if possible. When a trump card is led, play a higher trump card than the previous player if possible. The person who plays the highest card of the suit led or the highest trump card takes the trick.

Your trumps.   Opponents' trumps

You lead ♥ K, so opponents must play ♥ 10 and ♥ A. This allows you to win the remaining trumps when you regain the lead.

Melds in Pinochle:

Flush (A-10-K-Q-J of trump)	150 points
Royal Marriage (K-Q of trump)	40 points
Plain Marriage (K-Q of other suit)	20 points
Pinochle (♠Q- ♥J)	40 points
100 Aces (♠A- ♦A- ♣A- ♥A)	100 points
80 Kings (♠K- ♦K- ♣K- ♥K)	80 points
60 Queens (♠Q- ♦Q- ♣Q- ♥Q)	60 points
40 Jacks (♠J- ♦J- ♣J- ♥J)	40 points
Dix (pronounced 'deece') (9 of trump)	10 points

(If you declare a flush, you may not also declare the royal marriage it contains.)

When two of the same card, say two ♠As, are played to a trick, the one played first is considered the higher of the two.

When play is over, points are counted in tricks as follows:

Ace	11
10	10
King	4
Queen	3
Jack	2
Nine	0

Last trick wins 10 points.

Scoring: If you make your bid, collect points from each opponent according to the following scoring table. If you concede, lose points to each opponent according to the scoring table. If you play the hand and miss your bid, lose double to each opponent for going bête (pronounced 'bait').

Bid	Points
250–290	5
300–340	10
350–390	15
400–440	25
450–490	50
500+	100

For bids over 300, spades score double.

Example: You bid 370, and make 405, in spades. You receive 30 points from each opponent. If you had bid 400 and made 405 in spades, you'd win 50 from each. But, if you'd bid 410 and made only 405, you'd go bête in spades and lose 100 points to each opponent.

Tips: Don't count on the widow to provide you the melding help you need. There's just better than a one-in-six chance that one particular card will be there. Even when either of two cards will work, you've only got a one-in-three chance.

In calculating the points you'll lose in play, figure that each opponent may put a high card on your losing tricks.

As defenders, remember the cards you've seen the bidder meld that you can beat. These are cards you should be sure to win.

Variations: Other bidding practices have their own tradition. In one, after two passes the dealer must take with a bid of at least 250. Another format allows the dealer to pass out the hand, or to open it at 290 (but not at 250) or at 320 or higher. A third popular treatment is to require the first hand to start at 300, and be allowed to throw the hand in for the minimum-stake loss.

In *Four-Handed Partnership Pinochle,* partners sit facing each other. Deal 12 cards each, three at a time. Turn up the last card as the trump suit. If it's a 9, dealer scores 10 points. Otherwise, whoever first has a 9 may replace it with the trump upcard. Players in turn table their melds, which are recorded. Cards are picked up, and the player at the dealer's left begins by leading any card. Partners pool their tricks taken, and at the end of play count their points (last trick counts 10). The deal rotates. Game is played to 1000 points.

BEZIQUE

Bezique, the forerunner of Pinochle, was invented in the early 1800s in Sweden. By the 1850s, it was a hit all across Europe, and it soon arrived in America. It's still widely enjoyed in Britain, where score is kept with individual Bezique markers.

Number of players: two

Object: to score points by melding and by taking tricks containing aces and 10s (brisques)

The cards: Shuffle two sets of 32 cards, consisting of aces through 7s, together into one 64-card deck. Cards rank—from high to low—A-10-K-Q-J-9-8-7.

To play: Deal eight cards to each player (in groups of three, two, and three), and then turn up a card to designate the trump suit. Place that card faceup and slightly sticking out from under the draw pile. If the trump upcard is a 7, the dealer scores 10 points immediately.

Melds in Bezique:

Trump marriage (K-Q)	40 points
Nontrump marriage (K-Q in same suit)	20 points
Trump flush (A-10-K-Q-J)	250 points
Bezique (♠Q-♦J)	40 points
Double Bezique (♠Q-♦J-♠Q-♦J)	500 points
Any four aces	100 points
Any four kings	80 points
Any four queens	60 points
Any four jacks	40 points
7 of trump (each)	10 points

The nondealer leads any card to start play. At this stage of play, and as long as there remain

Hearts are trump. The ♥K and ♥Q form a 40-point marriage. On a later turn, if you are able to add the ♥A-♥10-♥J, you can score another 250 points for the trump flush. Remember that you can make only one meld per turn, and only if you've just won a trick.

Example of early play: You're dealt ♦ Q, ♦ 7, ♥ J, ♥ J, ♣ A, ♠ A, ♠ 10, ♠ Q, with the ♦ K upcard. Your first plan is to win a trick in order to exchange your ♦ 7 for the ♦ K, letting you immediately meld a 40-point trump marriage (♦ K- ♦ Q). You don't want to waste the ♠ A, a good melding card, to try to take an early trick. You might try the ♠ 10, but a less risky choice is one of your ♥ Js, which will likely win the trick if your opponent doesn't have a ♥ 10.

cards to draw, you are not obliged to follow suit, but may play any of your cards.

The highest trump card in a trick wins it, or, if there is no trump card, the highest card of the suit led wins it. When two identical cards contend for the same trick (for example, two ♥ 10s), the first one played wins the trick.

The winner of each trick scores 10 points for each ace or 10 (brisque) it contains, and may also table any one meld. (You may tally the 10 points for a 7 of trump along with another meld, and if you meld the first 7 of trump you may also exchange it for the trump upcard.) Tally all points as you score them.

Both players take a new card from the stock. The winner of the previous trick draws first and then leads to the next trick.

Melded cards stay on the table until the stock is used up, but you may still play them on tricks. A card you meld one time can be used again, but only in a different meld. For example: ♣ Q

melds with ♣ K in a marriage and can also meld later for 60 points with ♥ Q- ♦ Q- ♠ Q. But the marriage can't meld with a second ♣ K—a completely new pair is needed to score the second marriage.

When only the upcard and one draw card remain, the upcard goes to the trick-loser. Put your remaining melded cards back in your hand, with the winner of the previous trick taking the last draw card and leading to the next trick. In the play of the final eight cards, however, each player must follow suit and also must win a trick whenever possible. Whoever wins the final trick scores an extra 10 points. (See page 10 for an example of taking the last eight tricks.)

Scoring: The first player to accumulate 1000 points, or any other agreed upon sum, wins.

Tips: The play in Bezique has 32 tricks, most of which occur when your opponent can legally trump any ace or 10 you lead. Therefore, you should save your 10s to win lower cards when your opponent leads. Meanwhile, there's usually

Your hand.　　　　　　　　　　　Opponent's hand.

The last eight tricks of a Bezique hand. Here, diamonds are trump and it's your lead. If you lead ♥ 10, followed by ♠ J and ♠ 8, you'll win the brisques for the ♥ 10s and should also score 10 for last trick with a high trump. See what happens if you start with the ♣ K or ♣ Q: You'll lose the lead before playing your ♥ 10, and then your opponent can win both ♥ 10 brisques and the last trick!

a difficult suit for your opponent to win tricks in. Even if you lead low cards of that suit, it may cause discomfort: Players want to hold on to melding cards (aces, kings, queens, the 10 and jack of trump, and ♠ Q and ♦ J for a possible 500-point double bezique). Yet each player can hold just eight cards!

If you have a big meld near the end of the game—for example, ♠ Q-♠ Q-♦ J-♦ J—you may not have time to meld it in two stages to score an extra 40 points. Your opponent may see through that plan and prevent you from winning a second trick and the additional 500 points.

Variations: *Rubicon Bezique* uses 128 cards (a double Bezique pack) and emphasizes melding. Deal nine cards each. Trump is fixed by the first marriage melded instead of by turning a trump

card up, and new melds include triple bezique (1500 points), quadruple bezique (4500 points), and backdoor (nontrump A-10-K-Q-J), which counts 150 points.

Every deal is scored independently. The last trick counts 50. No one bothers with brisques, unless the loser needs the brisque points to get over 1000 points to avoid being rubiconned. The winner of a rubicon game scores a 1000-point bonus instead of 500, gets 320 points for brisques, and gets all of opponent's other points too!

If you're dealt a carte blanche (no picture cards), show it and score 50 points, and score 50 more after each draw until you do get a picture card!

You can remake a meld merely by replacing a played melded card!

CANASTA

Canasta—named for the Spanish word for "basket"—spread across Latin America in the 1940s. In 1950s, the game swept like wildfire across the United States. Now, nearly a half-century later, Canasta may do so once again.

Number of players: four, in partnerships seated across the table

Object: to score points by melding, with the goal of scoring a canasta and then going out

The cards: Use two regular packs of 52 cards plus their four jokers. Jokers and deuces are wild.

Melding: Melds must consist of at least three cards, all of the same rank. All melds are placed faceup on the table, and partners build up their melds together to form canastas—seven-card bonus melds. All jokers and deuces are wild and can be used in melds as any desired rank except 3s. A canasta must consist of at least four natural cards but may contain any number of wild cards.

The treys: Red 3s are bonus cards worth 100 points each, but they are not used in play. You should lay down a red 3 as soon as you can. If your side scores all four red 3s, the bonus for them doubles to 800 points.

Black 3s are used in play but are meldable only when going out (see "Going out"). Otherwise, they function as stopper cards (see "Freezing the pack").

To play: Deal 11 cards to each player, one at a time, and then turn over an upcard that starts a discard pile, or a pack. The remainder of the cards form the stock. *Note:* If the upcard is a wild card or a red 3, turn another card up on top of it, and see "Freezing the pack."

The player at the dealer's left goes first, with play passing in clockwise rotation until the hand is over. At your turn, even on the first round of play, you may take the pack with an appropriate hand of cards (see "Taking the pack"), but your usual turn consists of drawing one card and then discarding one card.

Initial melds: The first player to meld for a side must table at least 50 points of meld. All cards have point values for melding.

Joker	50 points
Deuce	20 points
Ace	20 points
King through 8	10 points
7 through 4	5 points
Black 3s	5 points

To calculate the value of a meld, simply add up the value of the cards it contains. Note that a three-card (or longer) meld must have at least two natural cards.

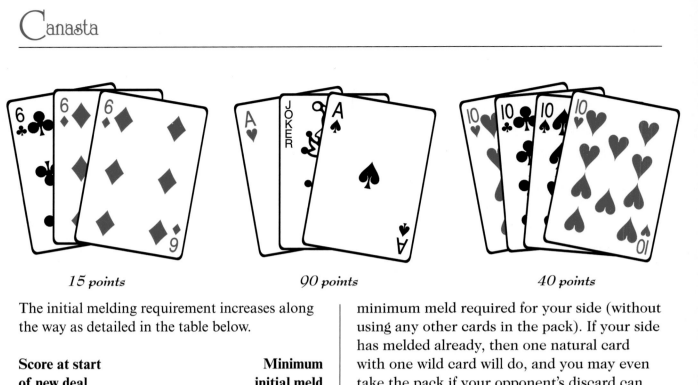

15 points   *90 points*   *40 points*

The initial melding requirement increases along the way as detailed in the table below.

Score at start of new deal	Minimum initial meld
Less than 0	15 points
0–1495	50 points
1500–2995	90 points
3000 or more	120 points

minimum meld required for your side (without using any other cards in the pack). If your side has melded already, then one natural card with one wild card will do, and you may even take the pack if your opponent's discard can go in one of your melds.

Also, once your side has met its initial meld, you may use the pack to form new melds or add to

You don't have to take the pack to make an initial meld, but it gives you more cards to play with. Wait until there are enough cards (around 10 or 12) in the pack to take it, so you will have more cards in your hand. In this case, taking the upcard gives you enough for a 60-point meld: ♥J- ♦J-♣J + ♠5- ♥5-♣2.

Taking the pack: You are allowed to take the pack—the entire current pile of discards—as long as you can meld the top discard and meet the following conditions: If your side hasn't melded yet, you'll need two natural cards to meld with the upcard, and you must meet the

your melds to form canastas, as you wish. Any cards you don't meld become part of your hand.

Once a meld is on the table, either partner may play off it. When a meld contains seven or more cards, it becomes a canasta. It is squared into a pile and a red card is placed on top if it consists of all natural cards (a natural canasta). A black card is placed on top if it contains any wild cards (a mixed canasta). If any wild cards are later added to a red canasta, it becomes a black canasta, and its value changes accordingly.

Going out: You go out (sometimes called going rummy) if you meld all the cards in your hand. However, in order to go out, your side has to have at least one canasta, and in most games you need one card left over to discard. Play ceases at this point, and the score for the hand is tallied.

Displaying a red card on top of the meld denotes a natural canasta (500 points, no wild cards), while a black card—if available—signals a mixed canasta (300 points, one to three wild cards).

Freezing the pack: Freezing the pack makes it difficult for any player to take the pack. To freeze the pack, discard a wild card sideways across the discards. The next player can't take the pack as long as a wild card remains. To pick up a frozen pack, you'll need a natural pair in your hand. This rule applies to all players, regardless of who froze the pack initially.

A black 3 freezes the pack momentarily, except in the unlikely event that a player with two black 3s can go out while taking the pack. That would require using every card taken in the pack. (You cannot meld wild cards with black 3s.)

When the player discards one card faceup on the pack, a turn is complete.

Before going out, you are allowed to ask your partner, "May I go out?" but you must abide by the answer. Should no one go out, the hand ends when the stock is gone, and no player can take the pack.

Scoring: Total the value of all melded cards and add bonuses for going out (100), natural canastas (500), mixed canastas (300), and red 3s (100 each, but 800 for all four). Subtract the total of cards retained in each player's hand (red 3s count –200 points), and tally each team's score. Game is 5000 points.

Tip: When taking the pack, don't meld everything in it immediately. Hold some cards back so you'll have natural pairs to take a frozen pack.

CASINO

Casino has descended to us directly from Scopa, the old Italian game. Widely enjoyed as a two- or three-handed game, Casino is also entertaining for four players—either as partners or "cutthroat" style.

Number of players: two to four

Object: to score points by winning cards in play by matching, combining, and building

The cards: Use a regular pack of 52 cards.

To play: Deal four cards facedown to each player and four to the table faceup. Keep the remaining cards for later rounds. The player at the dealer's left plays the first card of each round, with play continuing in clockwise order. When all players have played their four cards, the same dealer deals four more cards to each player. Cards are dealt to the table only in the first round.

At your turn, you might simply place a card on the table (see "Trailing"). However, there are several ways to take cards—or to try to take them: by matching, by combining, by building, and by taking another player's build.

You can combine the card you play with the cards on the table in many possible ways. Suits do not matter.

A Casino hand (top) and table layout (bottom).

Matching: If your card matches the rank of a card on the table, you can take the pair immediately, placing them in your own stack facedown in front of you. In the illustrated hand, you can take the ♥Q with the ♣Q, or you can take the ♠7 with the ♦7. Face cards match in pairs only, for example, when two kings are on the table and you hold one king in your hand, you capture only one of the kings. However, if three kings are dealt to the table, whoever has the fourth king takes them all. Plain cards can match in greater numbers.

Combining: If your card equals the combined sum of two or more cards on the table, you can take the cards immediately. In the deal shown, you may combine the ♣6 and ♣2 and take them away with the ♦8.

Building: If at least one card on the table plus the card you play totals another card in your hand, announce this build number and pile the build-cards together. In the example shown, play the ♠A onto the ♠7, and say, "Building 8s." You may also put the ♣6 and ♣2 into this build, making it a multiple build. On your next turn—if no one's taken your build—you can pick it up with your ♦8. (And, if you have no other build or capture, you must.) At your turn, you can take an opponent's build when you have the right card, and, of course, an opponent can take yours as well.

Occasionally, with the right holding, you can increase an opponent's build. With a deuce and a 10, play the deuce on top of a simple 8-build and announce, "Building 10s." Multiple builds, by the way, can't be built up to a higher number.

Trailing: If you have nothing else to do on your turn, you must trail a card—place it on the table without building it onto another card. You cannot do this if you have made a build that's still on the table.

When dealing the last round, call "Last" to alert the other players. Whoever takes the final cards on the last round also wins any untaken cards remaining at the end.

Scoring: Players count their cards and note the cards with extra value. Each game has 11 points.

♦10 (Big Casino)	2 points
♠2 (Little Casino)	1 point
Each ace	1 point
Spades (Whoever takes the most spades)	1 point
Cards (Whoever takes the most cards)	3 points

When there's a tie for cards in a two-player game, neither player scores. In a three-handed game, tied players score 2 points each; in a four-handed game, tied players score 1 point each.

Play to 21 points, or to any other agreed-upon number.

Tips: The more players in a game, the riskier it is to build. In a four-handed game, someone is likely to take a build made early in the round, so try to delay your build, if possible.

The fewer players in a game, the more you can control the action. It will help to know which key cards remain—10s, aces, and other high building cards. A skilled player in a two-handed game knows which cards have been played and which cards are left for the final round.

Variations: In *Scoops,* 1 point is scored for a scoop—a play that clears the table. Signify scoops by facing one card up for each scoop.

Continuous Casino: Deal as in regular Casino, but leave the stock of undealt cards in everybody's reach. In this game, take a new card after each play. No further rounds of cards are dealt. (This method can accommodate five players.)

Partnership Casino: Teammates sit across from each other, keeping winnings together and trying, within the rules, to help each other.

CONCENTRATION

The most appropriately named game of all time! "Concentration" is what you'll need to win this game. Since children sometimes are better at this game than adults are, it can be an enjoyable pastime for the entire family.

Number of players: two or more

Object: to gather in the most cards by matching them in pairs

The cards: Use a regular pack of 52 cards.

To play: You'll need a large surface area. Deal the whole deck out, card by card, facedown. It doesn't matter if the cards are in neat rows or in a haphazard arrangement.

These two cards don't match, but remember where they are for later play!

By tradition, the youngest player goes first. Each turn consists of turning up one card and then another, taking care to keep them in place. When the two cards match in rank, put them in your winnings pile and continue your turn, revealing two new cards.

However, when the cards you turn over are of different rank, your turn ends. Return them to their places, facedown. Try to concentrate on remembering where each card lies, as you may still pair one or the other later.

Scoring: When the cards have all been matched, record the number of cards you've taken. Whoever has the most cards after three games wins.

Tip: Concentration rewards visual recall, and some people are just better at this than others. This tip can help you keep pace: Say you've just seen another player turn the ♥5 and you suspect you remember the location of a 5 seen earlier. When your turn comes, go first for the earlier 5, not for the ♥5. When you're right, all you have to do is grab the ♥5 (but don't forget where it is). This way, if the first card you turn over is not a 5, you've still got a chance to find a match.

Variations: With a very young crowd of players, you may want to omit some cards for a smaller layout. For example, you may wish to leave out all aces, 3s, 5s, 7s, and 9s.

For a more advanced crowd, play *Moving Concentration:* You may return pairs that don't match to new spots in the layout!

Coon Can

A game that originated down South, Coon Can comes from the Spanish ¿con quién? (meaning "with whom?"). Also known as Conquian, it is one of the few rummy games that has lasted over a century. Perhaps its colorful lingo contributes to its long-term appeal.

Number of players: two

Object: to go coon can, that is to meld all your cards, plus an extra card you pick from the draw or discard pile

The cards: Use a 40-card pack (akin to a Spanish pack) or a standard pack with all 10s, 9s, and 8s

Coon Can's Terminology

Hit (noun): a card laid off on a meld

Hit (verb): to lay a card off on a meld

Hole: a hand you can't go coon can with

Long spread: suit sequence meld

Pluck: to pick a card from stock

Short spread: meld of the same rank

Sleep it: to purposely overlook a play

Switch: to move a card from one meld to another

removed. This leaves the jack and 7 in sequence. Aces are low.

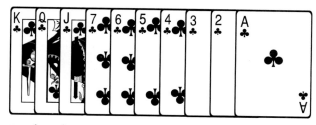

Rank order in Coon Can.

Melding: Melds in Coon Can must have at least three cards and are left on the table.

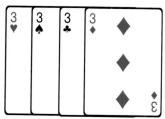

Short spreads.

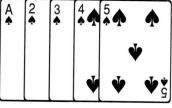

Long spreads.

To play: Deal ten cards each and leave the rest facedown as a draw pile, or stock. The nondealer begins by plucking (turning up) and showing the top card from stock. You cannot add a plucked card to your hand, so if this card is not used in a meld, it must be discarded. Each player in turn must either take the top discard and meld it, or turn up the top card from stock and add it to a spread or discard it.

During one turn, you may hit your own spreads with any number of cards, but when you hit your opponent's spread, that's considered your

Occasionally, no one goes coon can—a tab game—and the stake for it is added to the next game.

Tips: A good amount of skill is involved in hitting your opponent with the intent of forcing a discard from his or her hand. This discard may

In Coon Can, you can move cards from one meld to another (switch) as long as you leave legal spreads.

discard. When your spread is hit by your opponent, you have 11 cards. You must discard from your hand instead of plucking a new card!

You may shift your own melds around to create new melds as long as you leave valid melds behind.

Forcing: Opponent shows these two spreads. When you hit with ♥ Q, it forces the discard of one of the two concealed cards.

If you go coon can (have 11 cards in spreads), the game ends and you win the agreed stake.

be a card you can use, or it may spoil your adversary's plans. Also, you may be able to force your opponent into a hole—a hand that can't go coon can. For instance, a hand that's a ten-card-long spread (a spread of an entire suit, for example) can't go coon can, since an eleventh card is required.

Sleeping it: Discarding a card that could match one's own spread may often be a good strategy, but it can be stopped. When you see your opponent sleeping it, you may force your opponent to hit with it instead, forcing a further discard.

Variations: People who are uncomfortable with placing a 7 and jack in sequence may instead use a 40-card pack, aces through 10s, removing all face cards.

Some games permit players to pluck a card just "on speculation," rather than requiring it to be immediately melded or added to a spread.

CRAZY EIGHTS

Eights are wild and so is the action in this fast-paced game the whole family can play. An easy-to-learn game that calls for a lot of luck, Crazy Eights is a very good game to play with kids.

Number of players: two to six (Even more can play, but the more players, the longer each person has to wait between turns.)

Object: to be the first player to get rid of all your cards

The cards: Use a regular pack of 52 cards, but with four or more players you might want to use two packs!

To play: Deal seven cards each, turn one card up to start a discard pile, and leave the remainder of the cards next to the pile as a draw stack, or stock. The player at the dealer's left begins by covering the upcard with a matching card—one that's either the same suit or same rank. For example, if the starter is ◆ 7, you can play any diamond or any 7. When you can't match, draw cards from stock until you find a match.

All 8s are wild and you can play them at any time. Call the 8 any suit; the next player must match it. (Don't specify a rank.)

It's your turn to match the ♥ 4. Choose ♣ 4, ♥ Q, or ♥ 9. Save the wild card (◆ 8) for when you really need it!

Play rotates to the left, as each player matches the top card, and continues until one player has no cards left. If you run out of draw cards along the way, simply turn the discard pile facedown, shuffle well, and use it for a new draw pile.

Scoring: Whoever goes out scores the point total of cards left in everyone else's hands. Each 8 counts 50, face cards count 10, and all others count their face value (ace = 1). The game usually ends after an agreed time limit or number of deals.

Tips: When you have many cards of one suit, others may find that suit hard to match. Remember, in a game with several players, your play affects the next player most.

Don't get caught holding wild cards at the end of play, since they count a whopping 50 points each!

Variations: In *Double Crazy Eights,* turn the upcard sideways so that two piles can fit on it. As play goes on, you may choose which pile to play on. You may still play an 8 anytime, but you must match it next by its own suit.

CRIBBAGE

This appealing game, which has been played for more than 350 years, is in a class by itself. It may take you a few moments to learn, but once you pick it up you'll begin to admire its many chances for thought and strategy. Since scoring occurs at nearly every moment, a cribbage board is very useful.

Number of players: two to four (The two-handed game is described first.)

Object: to score points for certain card combinations and be the first to peg 121 points (or 61, as agreed)

The cards: Use a regular pack of 52 cards. Each card has a point value equal to its rank. Aces are low and count 1. Face cards count 10.

To play: Deal six cards to each player. Both players then select two cards to discard for a facedown, four-card crib belonging to the dealer. The goal is to retain a hand of four cards that will form scoring combinations.

The dealer lays the crib aside without looking at it, and it is not used until after the play.

Scoring combinations:

Fifteen (any combination of cards totaling exactly 15)	2 points
Pair (two cards of the same rank)	2 points
Triplet (three cards of the same rank)	6 points
Quartet (four cards of the same rank)	12 points
Sequence (three or more cards in a row, any suit)	1 point per card
Flush (any four cards of the same suit)	1 point per card
His Nobs (jack of the starter's suit, in hand)	1 point

Note that flushes and His Nobs don't score during play.

Next, the nondealer cuts the pack and the dealer turns up the top card (the start or starter). If the

Nondealer selects ♥8, ♦K to discard for the crib. Dealer selects ♠5, ♠J to discard for the crib.

start is a jack, the dealer scores 2 points for His Nobs. The starter card is not used in play. The remaining cards form the stock, which is not used in this hand.

The nondealer plays one card faceup, calling out its value. The dealer does the same, calling the total of the two cards played. Continue as long as the count doesn't exceed 31. Keep cards in two separate piles—one for the dealer's cards, one for the nondealer's cards. When you can't play without exceeding 31, say, "Go," which instructs your opponent to continue play without going past 31, as opponent pegs 1 for your go. If your opponent is able to reach 31 exactly after your go, he or she pegs 2 instead of

the fourth one scores 12. Sequences also count, and the cards don't have to be in exact order. Example: 3-6-4-5 scores 4 points for the last player, and if the next player follows with a deuce, that sequence is worth 5 points. A flush (series of cards of the same suit) does not score in play; it scores only when scoring the hand.

Scoring the hands: After you play out the cards, the nondealer's hand is counted and pegged (see "Scoring combinations"), followed by the dealer's hand, and then the dealer's crib. This order is important because if at any point either player reaches 121 (or 61), the game is immediately ended. The start card is scored as a fifth card in each hand.

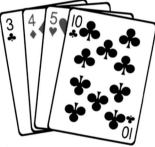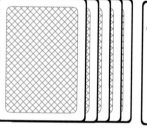

Nondealer starts by saying, "Three." Dealer plays the ♠ 8 and says, "11." Nondealer plays ♦ 4 and says, "15 for 2," while pegging 2. This is followed by "23," "28," "29," and "go." Dealer also cannot play under 31 but pegs 1 for the nondealer's go. Nondealer begins the new count by playing the ♣ 10 and calling, "Ten." "Sixteen and last," says the dealer, pegging 1.

1 (1 for 31, 1 for go). When you both are unable to play, the player who didn't make the last play begins a new count. Playing the last card of all counts 1 point.

Pegging for melds made in play: Cards must be played consecutively within one 31-count to score. In addition to scoring for go, 31, and the last card, combinations made during play also score points. If your play makes the count 15, score 2. If you match the rank of the card played by your opponent, score 2 for the pair. Three cards of the same rank are worth 6 points, and

In the illustrated hand (above), the nondealer pegs 12: two sequences (3-4-5, 3-4-5), one pair (3s), and two 15s (5-10, 3-3-4-5). Dealer pegs 6: two 15s (8-6-A, 8-6-A) and a pair (8s). By custom, the nondealer now separates the start card, gathers in the rest, and the dealer pegs the crib. In this case, (see page 20) it's worth 5: two 15s (5-J, 5-K) and His Nobs (♠ J).

At the end of each hand, all the cards (from the dealer's hand, the nondealer's hand, the crib, and the stock) are gathered and shuffled together to form a fresh pack of 52 for the next hand. The

The board has 30 holes in each of the long rows, marked off in groups of five. Each player gets two pegs. In the beginning, the four pegs sit at the start end of the board. The pegs move up the outside and down the inside back to the start, for a total of 61 points. The usual game is two trips, or 121 points. The two pegs are used alternately, the back peg leapfrogging over the front peg.

nondealer from the last hand becomes the dealer for new hand.

Pegging out: When you peg to 121 (or to 61, as agreed), the game ends, no matter when this occurs. If the loser fails to score at least 61 points in a game of 121, he or she is skunked, or lurched, and the winner scores for a double game.

Tips: In play, start with a card under 5 so that the next player can't peg a quick 2 points for 15. Hold back your low cards to help score for go or 31. Also, keep an eye open for surprise sequences. For instance, if the first cards are a 6 and a 2, and a 3, 4, and 5 are the next cards (in any order), peg 5 points!

Keep in mind who gets the crib when you contribute to it. Pairs or 5s put in your own crib can be better than holding them, but give your opponent high and low cards—such as a queen and a 2.

Near the end of the game, desperate strategies may be necessary. For example, if you are the dealer and both you and your opponent need a few points to win, you'll need to peg out in play, since your opponent's hand scores ahead of yours. Therefore, keep cards that can score points in play—forget about making a high-scoring hand.

Variations: If your opponent fails to peg for a score, call, "Muggins," and peg the points yourself. Friendly games often omit this rule.

Cribbage for Three: Each player competes independently. If you're using a cribbage board, two players will have to peg up and down a single line of pegging-holes.

Deal five cards to each player and one card to the crib. Each player then chooses one card to add to the crib. For the start card, the dealer offers either adversary the cut. Player at the dealer's left then starts play, which proceeds clockwise. Go still scores 1 point; and if two players in succession say, "Go," it still pegs 1. (With three players, you may receive a point for go and later in the same count say, "Go," yourself.)

Cribbage for Four: Although this can be played cutthroat style—each player on his or her own—more commonly it's a partnership game, played with the partners facing each other.

Deal five cards to each player. Each player then donates one card to the crib. Only one player pegs for each side, with the cribbage board placed between these two players. Partners may, however, point out counts or melds to each other.

DEMON

This is a solitaire game played by many people at once, with everybody building on common piles. Action and noise can reach high levels, so you may need to keep a whistle handy!

Number of players: two to eight

Object: to play out more cards than any other player

The cards: Use a regular pack of 52 cards per player. Each pack should have a different back design.

To play: Each player deals a layout for the solitaire widely known as Klondike (called Canfield in England). Refer to the diagram below for the proper layout.

Wait for all players to complete their layouts. At a signal, turn over three cards from stock to start your waste heap, and begin making plays. Once the game is underway, play at your own pace.

There are several moves available to you. You should release your aces into the center of the table as soon as possible, where any player can build them up in sequence by suit, ending with the king. These piles are called foundation piles. Play cards onto the center foundation piles as available. Note that everyone can play onto each foundation pile, but each player can only play onto his or her own layout.

You can build downward sequences on the cards in your layout, in alternating suit color only. For example, the ♥10 can be moved upon the ♣J, but not on the ♦J. In the illustrated hand, move the ♦8 onto the ♠9, move both to the ♥10, and move these to the ♣J. All of these end up on the ♥Q! You're left with one empty pile and three new cards to turn up.

To achieve this layout, first deal a row of seven cards with the leftmost one faceup and the rest facedown. On top of the facedown cards, deal another row, with the leftmost of these faceup. Keep doing this until you have seven piles, ranging from one card on the left to seven cards on the right, with the top cards faceup. The remainder of the cards form the stock.

When you move a card from its pile, turn up the card beneath. Occasionally a pile empties, opening up a vacancy. You can fill this only with a king or with a sequence headed by a king.

The topmost card of your waste heap is always available for play, as is any single card on a pile, and also the topmost (lowest) card of a sequence.

When you've gone through the stock, three cards at a time, turn your waste heap over to make a new stock. You can continue to do this as often as you like. At some point you may run out of plays, but as other players develop their layouts, your cards may become eligible to play in the center, and you may find several more plays.

The game ends when one player's cards have all been played onto the middle foundation piles. That player shouts, "Demon," and all further play ceases. The cards on the foundation piles are then sorted out and returned to each player. (The game is also considered ended when no player can find a play.)

Scoring: A player going out scores 52 points plus a 10-point bonus, and everyone else gets 1 point per card in the foundation piles. One player keeps a tally for everyone, and at the end of an agreed upon number of deals the winner is the one with the highest total score.

Note: Not infrequently, two players will attempt to play the same card on the same foundation pile. Whoever's card is at the bottom is deemed to have gotten there first.

Tips: Fast action is a key to winning, so set yourself up to make quick consecutive plays to the foundation piles.

Keep the center orderly by turning over the foundation piles that have been completely built up to a king.

To keep the game alive, you may point out plays to another player.

Variation: Play solitaires other than Klondike that offer common scoring piles for all players.

EUCHRE

Euchre is thought to have descended directly from Triomphe, an immensely popular sixteenth-century game. A hundred years ago in America, Euchre had plenty of devotees and was considered our national game!

Number of players: four, with partners seated facing each other (Euchre may also be played by two or three players.)

Object: to score points by winning at least three of five tricks

The cards: Use a 32-card pack, aces through 7s for each suit. All 2s through 6s are discarded before play. Cards rank as follows: A-K-Q-J-10-9-8-7, except in a trump suit, where the jack—called the right bower—is the highest trump, and the other jack of the same color—the left bower—is the second highest trump.

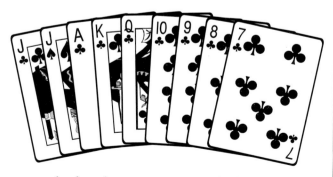

Rank of cards in trump suit, with clubs trump.

To play: Deal five cards to each player, in bunches of two and three, or three and two, and turn up the next card to propose a trump suit. If that suit becomes the trump suit, the upcard replaces another in the dealer's hand. By custom, it stays on the table, while the card it replaces is put beneath the remaining undealt cards.

Determining the trump suit: Starting at the dealer's left, each player has a chance to accept or pass the suit turned as trump. To accept, an opponent of the dealer says, "I order it up," the dealer's partner says, "I assist," and the dealer accepts by discarding. Any player may pass.

On balance, to accept you should judge your side at least a two-to-one favorite, since you win only 1 point when you succeed (unless you score a march), but lose 2 points when you fail (see "Scoring").

If all four players pass, the dealer places the upcard under the pack of undealt cards, and another round to find a trump suit follows. Starting with the player at the dealer's left, each may pass until one player names a trump suit other than the suit first turned up. If all players again pass, throw the cards in for a new deal.

When accepting or naming a trump suit, you may also declare at that time to play alone. Your partner's hand is put aside, and you play against both opponents.

The player at the dealer's left usually leads to the first trick, but when you play a lone hand, the defender at your left leads first.

On each trick, follow the suit of the card led if possible. Otherwise, play any card. Each trick is won by the highest card of the suit led, except a trick containing trump cards, which is won by the highest trump played. Note that the ♥ J is not considered a heart when diamonds are trump!

Scoring:

Declaring side wins three or four tricks   1 point
Declaring side wins five tricks (a march) 2 points
If lone hand wins   4 points
Declaring side euchred (wins fewer than
    three tricks), opponents score   2 points
Game is played to a predetermined number of points, usually 5, 7, or 10.

Tips: The trump suit has nine cards, but there are only seven cards in the other suit of the same color. The two remaining suits have eight cards each. Since each deal leaves out about a third of the deck, on average only five or six cards of each suit are in play. If you have three cards from the trump suit and your partner can take a trick, you are likely to win the majority of tricks.

When you have three winning cards in your hand and chances of winning the other cards, it may be wise to play alone. Your nontrump cards, even if not clear winners, may take tricks: Your opponents have only ten cards between them, and may fail to hold on to the right cards!

Don't forget that if the upcard is accepted as the trump suit, it becomes part of the dealer's hand. This may influence your decision to accept that suit as trump for your side.

The game score may also influence your decision to pass, accept, or play alone. If you have a large lead, it may be a good risk to venture a questionable acceptance of the trump suit if you fear an opponent may score a march (4 points) in a different suit. Even if you're euchred, opponent scores only 2 points.

Variations: *Two-Handed Euchre* is generally played with a 24-card pack, omitting 7s and 8s. Score for a march is 2 points, and the option to declare a lone hand does not exist.

Three-Handed Euchre: The player who makes trump plays against the other two, who temporarily unite as partners. The scoring is as follows:

Maker of trump suit wins three
    or four tricks   1 point
Maker of trump suit wins
    five tricks (a march)   3 points
Maker of trump suit is euchred,
    each opponent wins   2 points

Railroad Euchre: A joker is added as the highest trump card, regardless of suit.

FAN TAN

Don't confuse Fan Tan—also known as Card Dominoes, Sevens, and Parliament—with Chinese Fan Tan, an unrelated gambling game.

Number of players: three to eight (The game is best when four play.)

Object: to be the first to play off all your cards

The cards: Use a regular pack of 52 cards. Aces are low.

To play: Give each player an equal supply of chips; you'll need a bowl or a dish to collect chips for the kitty. Deal one card at a time to each player, until the whole pack is dealt. It doesn't matter if some players have one card fewer than the others.

Beginning with the player at the dealer's left, each player must play a 7, or else add on to cards in suit-sequences ascending or descending from the 7s.

Once the ◆ 7 has been played, for example, the ◆ 8 and ◆ 6 can be played. If the ◆ 8 is played, you can play the ◆ 9, and so on. Sequences ascend to the king and descend to the ace. Once an end card is reached, fold up the row of cards and turn them over.

Whenever you don't have a card to play, pass and toss one chip into the kitty. Whoever is out of cards first collects the chips in the kitty, plus one chip per card left in each player's hand.

Tips: Try to encourage play in suits where you have aces or kings. Your goal is to be able to hold back stoppers: the 5s, 6s, 8s, and 9s that block everyone else's cards but not your own. If your timing is right, the suits you need help in will open up before your stoppers are gone.

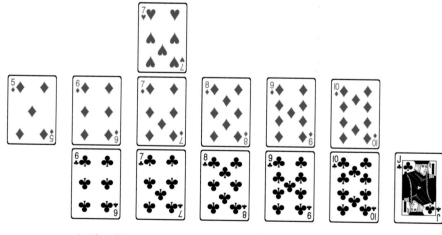

A Fan Tan game in progress after several plays.

GO FISH

For many of us, Go Fish was our first card game, and for some of us, it may still be the one we play best!

Number of players: two to six

Object: to win the most sets of four cards (books) by asking other players for them

The cards: Use a regular pack of 52 cards, but you might shorten the pack for a quicker game by removing all the cards of a few different ranks.

To play: When two people play, deal seven cards each; otherwise, deal five cards each. Leave the undealt cards facedown as a draw pile. Starting with the player at the dealer's left, each player asks another for cards of a specific rank. For example: "Kevin, do you have any 6s?" In order to ask, you yourself must already have at least one 6. Kevin has to give you all the 6s he holds, but the other players do not.

Whenever your request for a card is filled, it remains your turn. Continue with your turn, asking any player for cards of a specific rank. When the player you ask can't oblige, you'll be told to "Go fish." Pick up the top card of the draw pile. If it's the rank you called for, show the card at once, and your turn goes on. Otherwise, your turn ends.

If this is your hand, you can ask for 6s, 3s, 8s, Ks, 9s, or aces.

Play proceeds to the left in this fashion. Whenever you have collected all four cards of one rank (a book), show the other players, then place the book next to you in a compact pile.

Scoring: When all the cards have been drawn and all the books collected, whoever has the most books wins.

Tip: Pay attention to who seeks which cards, for you will certainly draw a card someone was looking for earlier. You'll capture those cards at your next turn if you can remember which player to ask!

Variations: Call for cards from all players at once: The game moves faster when everyone must give up the wanted cards. This also makes it a better move to ask for a card when your book lacks just one, since whoever might have drawn the fourth one must give it to you.

An interesting scoring variant is to give each book a value equal to its rank. Aces can count 11, picture cards 10, and all others their face value.

Hearts

In any of its numerous versions, Hearts is not difficult to play, but it's certainly not easy to master. An observant and calculating player will be a consistent winner. Actually, Hearts is a game for the loser in us, for if you hold a lot of low cards, you'll win!

Point-scoring cards in Hearts. Try not to take these cards, or else try to take them all!

Number of players: four (However, three or six may also play. The four-player version is explained here.)

Object: to win as few of the penalty cards as possible (all the hearts as well as the ♠Q), or, if the hand is strong enough, to win them all

The cards: Use a regular pack of 52 cards. Aces are high.

To play: Deal cards one at a time, until each player has 13.

The pass: An interesting feature of Hearts is the pass, where each player sends three cards to another player before the opening lead. A popular method is to pass the cards to the left on the first deal, to the right on the second deal, and across on the third deal, with no pass at all on the fourth deal. The cycle then repeats. Players may not look at the cards passed to them until they have completed their own pass.

Whoever holds the ♣2 now leads it. Follow suit if possible but if you can't, play any card other than a heart or the ♠Q. Whoever plays the highest card of the suit led wins the trick and leads to the next. For example, whoever plays the highest club on the first trick takes the cards played to that trick, and leads to the next.

Breaking hearts: You can't lead a heart until hearts have been broken—that is, until someone has discarded a heart already. However, if it's your lead and all you have are hearts, you must lead one.

Scoring: After all the tricks have been played out, count up the penalty cards you've taken. Count 1 for each heart, and 13 for the ♠Q. For instance, if your tricks include the ♠Q and the ♥6, ♥7, ♥9, ♥10, and ♥K, you would receive 18 points. The other three players would score the remaining 8 points. Keep a running tally. The game ends when someone reaches 100

Your hand before a right-hand pass. You should pass the ♠Q, ♦9, and ♥6. With the ♠Q on your right, the ♠A is not a dangerous card! If you were passing left, you'd pass the ♠A instead of the ♥6.

points or any agreed upon sum. Whoever has the lowest score at the end is the winner.

Shooting the moon: If the tricks you win contain all the hearts and the ♠Q, this is called shooting the moon. Subtract 26 points from your score if you accomplish this. (If you choose, you may add 26 points to everyone else's score. This would end the game more quickly.)

Tips: You generally want to avoid taking tricks; however, on most hands, you'll take a few. Your main concern is always to avoid the trick that includes the ♠Q. This affects the pass especially. If you are dealt the ♠Q, you may be safer keeping it if you have at least five spades. Otherwise it may be a danger in your hand and you should pass it, for the other players will lead spades. The ♠A and ♠K are risky to keep when you are short of spades, since they may be forced to capture the dreaded ♠Q. Spades lower than the ♠Q are usually very safe to keep, since none can capture the ♠Q!

Sometimes it's best to pass all your cards in a short suit with no low cards, since you'd be forced to win tricks in that suit otherwise. On some hands it may be wise to pass cards in a

variety of suits, to increase the likelihood of everyone following suit.

If you are thinking of shooting the moon, pass away all hearts that might be losers, since suspicious players will not let you win any hearts of mid-rank if they suspect you're shooting.

Variations: There's practically an infinite number of ways that Hearts can be played, so make sure everyone is playing by the same rules. One popular rule is that the ♠Q must be discarded at its first available opportunity. This avoids accusations of a player holding it to dump on a specific opponent. Another widespread rule is to count either the ♦J or ♦10 as –10 points in favor of whoever wins it.

In some games, the pass is always to the left, while some prefer no pass at all; in others, the ♣2 isn't required to be led—instead, the player at the dealer's left may lead any card at all.

For three players, discard the ♦2, leaving 51 cards, and deal 17 cards to each player. Pass four cards, not three. With more or fewer than four players, you can pass left and right, but not across.

I Doubt It

I Doubt It is a hilarious game that is fun for children as well as adults. If you're the sneaky sort and have a suspicious mind, then this game is for you!

Number of players: two or more (It's a greater challenge with at least three players.)

Object: to be the first player to get rid of all your cards

The cards: Use a regular pack of 52 cards for two to five players. Use two packs of 52 cards for six or more players.

To play: Deal all the cards out, as evenly as possible. To save time, deal in twos or threes.

In turn, players discard one or more cards, announcing them by rank. Start with aces.

The player at the dealer's left begins by saying, for example, "Two aces," and placing two cards facedown in the center of the table to begin a discard stack.

The following player announces, "Deuces,"—or perhaps, "One deuce"—and puts a single card facedown on the stack. The next player announces, "3s," and so on, each player stating a rank just above the previous one. After you reach kings, start again at aces.

At your turn you must discard, but the cards you discard don't have to be the rank called for. You might announce, "Three queens," and discard two jacks and a 6, or any three cards. Be convincing. Anyone can challenge you by being first to shout, "I doubt it!"

Lay successive discard packets crosswise, to avoid disputes. Here, a player has announced four 7s but has been caught playing two 6s, a 3, and an 8!

The challenge: If challenged, turn over your discards. If they're not what you claimed, pick up the entire discard pack. But if your cards are as announced, your challenger picks up the stack!

Note that when you use a single pack, you can discard up to four cards. With a double deck, the discard can go as high as eight cards.

Tips: Often you'll need to make a phony discard. This may be easier to do when the discard stack is low. You may get away with a one-card lie.

As the pile grows, so do the risks of discarding and challenging. Also, you're sure to be challenged on your final discard. So, plan ahead to have at least one card of the rank you'll need.

KALUKI

Spell it Kalooki, Caloochi, Kalogghi, or whatever, but this double-deck rummy game has been a longtime club favorite in America and Great Britain.

Number of players: two to six

Object: to be the first player to get rid of all the cards in your hand by creating melds

The cards: Use two regular packs of 52 cards plus their four jokers. Aces are high or low, but not both.

To play: With two to four players, deal 15 cards each. With five players, deal 13 cards each, and with six players, deal 11 cards each. After all the cards are dealt, turn one card up to start the discard pile. Use the remaining cards to form the stock. A player cannot take the upcard until he or she has made an initial meld or can use the upcard immediately in a meld. Your first meld must total at least 51 points, which can include cards you lay off on other players' melds as long as you table at least one meld of your own.

Value of cards in melding:

Ace	15 points
Face card	10 points
Plain card	face value
Joker	value of the card it stands for

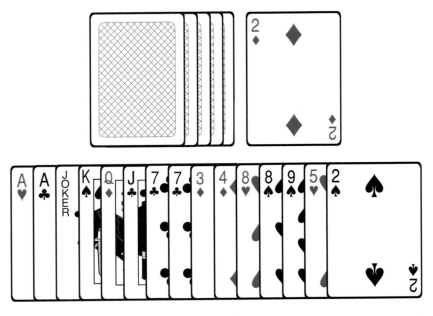

Pick up the ♦ 2 for a sequence (9 points), and use the joker as an ace, counting 15 (45 points). Since 9 + 45 = 54 points, you are able to meld. This doesn't take into account any layoffs you may be able to make.

Melds are three or more cards of the same rank (no repeated suits) or three or more cards of the same suit in sequence. Aces can be high or low, but not both. For example, ◆Q-◆K-◆A and ◆A-◆2-◆3 are valid melds, but ◆K-◆A-◆2 is not.

Before your initial meld, when it is your turn, either take the upcard if you can meld it, or else take the top card from the stock, meld if able, and discard. After your initial meld, you are entitled to pick up the card showing and discard from your hand without melding. Whenever you meld, you also have the option to lay off cards on your own melds, as well as other players' melds.

Scoring: Each losing player pays the winner 1 point per card left in hand, and 2 points per joker left in hand. A player who goes out on a single play goes Kaluki and collects double from every player.

Tips: Usually it doesn't take many rounds for someone to go out, so there's no real advantage to delaying your initial meld.

Jokers are valuable. While they can be melded as a group for 15 points each, they are put to much better use individually.

At your turn of play, you may swap a card for a joker that's melded as that card. In this meld, if you have the ◆9, exchange it for the joker, which you can use later however you choose.

Variations: In scoring, an alternate practice is to penalize players for the face value of the cards in their hand, with jokers counting 25 points each.

One version of Kaluki counts aces as 11, not 15, so agree among players about this beforehand.

The many names of this game—Chicago,

Saratoga, Newmarket, Stops, Boodle,

and others—show its far-reaching appeal.

Though played with cards and chips,

it involves no betting.

Number of players: two or more

Object: to win chips by being the first player out of cards, and also by playing money or boodle cards

The cards: Use a regular pack of 52 cards, plus an extra ♥A, ♣K, ♠Q, and ♦J (the boodle cards). Aces are high.

The layout of boodle cards.

To play: Distribute an equal number of chips to each player. Place the four boodle cards faceup in the center of the table, where they remain throughout play. Each player puts one chip on each boodle card.

Deal all the cards out, one at a time, dealing one hand more than players. For example, if there are four players, deal five hands. The extra hand, called the widow, is dealt to the dealer's left. It's all right if some players have one more card than others.

As the dealer, look at your cards and decide if you wish to exchange them for the widow (without seeing it first). If you prefer, keep your original hand and auction the widow, still unseen, to the other players. The auction begins at one chip. Collect the chips bid for it, and keep them in your own hand. The high bidder wins the widow hand and must play it, but this player retains an advantage in knowing which cards will be out of play.

The player at the dealer's left leads the lowest card held of any suit. Whoever has the next card in sequence in that suit plays it, and so on, until no one can play. For example, the ♥4 is led, the same player also plays the ♥5, and then other players follow with the ♥6, ♥7, and ♥8. No one has the ♥9, a stopper, so whoever played the ♥8 now continues play, leading the lowest card of a different suit.

When an ace is played, the sequence ends. As always, begin a new sequence with your lowest card in another suit. Whenever you play a

This hand has no boodle cards, no aces, and no other high cards to finish off the run of a suit. If this is your hand as dealer, swap it for the widow. If you're not the dealer, you should bid for the widow and get rid of this hand.

boodle card, collect the chips on it. If you play your last card, the deal ends and you win. Collect the remaining chips on the boodle cards and also one chip from each player for every card you catch them with.

The deal also ends when no one can play. If this happens, leave all uncollected chips on the boodle cards. The deal passes to the left, and all players put another chip on each boodle card. Since the dealer has an advantage, the game ends after an agreed number of dealt rounds. Whoever has the most chips wins.

Tip: If you take the widow, remember the cards you threw away. This can help a lot in the play.

Variations: As an alternative to bidding for a widow hand, some prefer to set aside several or more stop cards that no one sees.

Another version of Michigan makes players pay an extra penalty if they're caught at the end holding a boodle card.

Another variation adds a fifth boodle, usually the sequence ♥9-♥10-♥J. Add cards to the layout from another deck, and anyone playing two of these cards in a row collects their boodle chips.

You can always use an A-K-Q-J of different suits for boodle cards, by the way, but if you use the 9-10-J sequence boodle, it should be the same suit as the ace.

Here's the widow hand for which you traded the hand above. This is a much better hand! Let's say the game is started with the ♣7. You'll end the sequence with the ♣A, winning the ♣K boodle, and now, because you know which cards are out of the game, you can control the rest of play. Lead the ♥2. Since the ♥3 is a stopper, you go to a different suit, playing ♠4. The ♠5 is in the discards too, so you switch back to ♥6. This will play to your ♥9, again making a stop. Now the ♠J will play to your ♠A, and when you play the ♦8, the hand's over!

In Oh Hell!, it's not how good your cards are,

but how good your luck and judgment are.

The game does have its momentary upsets,

so if you need a name that's a bit more tame,

just call it "Oh Well!"

Number of players: three to seven (It is best with four or five players. One player should be scorekeeper.)

Object: to make precisely the number of tricks you bid—no more, and no less

The cards: Use a regular pack of 52 cards. Aces are high.

To play: A game of Oh Hell! consists of a series of rounds. On the first, deal each player one card; on the second, deal two cards; and on the third, deal three cards, increasing the deal by one card each hand until the top limit. For example, when four people play, deal 13 cards on the last round. With five players, deal ten cards on the last round. The deal goes to the left for each new round.

After dealing, turn up one card to designate the trump suit. If you turn over an ace or a deuce, however, play at no-trump, with no suit as trump. Also, whenever you deal all 52 cards, play at no-trump.

The bidding: Starting at the dealer's left, players state in turn the number of tricks they hope to win. The scorekeeper records each bid. The total number of tricks bid for on each deal must differ from the number of tricks available. Therefore,

In a five-handed game, you hold this hand. Bid "One." You'll take the ace of trump—it's a sure winner. If you're careful, you won't take another trick! Spades probably won't be led three times, and even so, the ♠ 10 shouldn't be a problem. The ♥ 5 is not likely to win, and the key will be to save the ♦ 3, a low trump, for a trick containing higher trump cards. An ideal scenario would be for a club to be led, so you could trump it with the ♦ A and then lead the ♦ 3.

the scorer must require the last bidder—the dealer—to register a legal bid.

Once all the bids are recorded, the player at the dealer's left leads any card desired. Always follow suit if possible, but play any card otherwise. Each trick is taken by the highest card in it of the suit led, or by the highest trump card if it contains any trump. The winner of each trick leads to the following trick.

Scoring: After all the tricks are taken, the scorekeeper tallies how everyone fared. If you made your bid exactly, score 1 point per trick plus a 10-point bonus. If you failed, however, subtract 10 points for each trick you're off, whether it's more or less than your bid. (Because of this, it's not unusual to end up with a negative score.) The player with the most points after the last deal wins.

Tips: Bidding in the first few rounds can be tricky, since so few cards from the pack are in play, and some bids are forced. In the early deals, you'll be surprised to see your low cards win tricks, while your aces get trumped. In most deals, you can count on low cards to be losers more reliably than counting on high cards to be winners (unless they're high trump cards).

When the bid-total is above the number of tricks in the deal, other players will be quite willing to capture your questionable middle-range cards or trump a trick that you have the high card on. However, when the bid-total is under the trick-total, players will be happy to let you win an extra trick or two.

Variations: Some players prefer to write down bids secretly. In this case, it's okay for the bid-total and the trick-total to turn out equal. Those bids can be revealed either before the first lead or after the last trick.

In many games, once the highest possible number of cards is dealt, the game continues with the number of cards per hand decreasing by one each hand, until a final one-card deal.

OLD MAID

Many of us think Old Maid requires a special pack of cards, but actually its ancestral form, some 150 years ago, likely used a regular pack minus one card.

Number of players: three or more (Although two can play.)

Object: not to be left holding the Old Maid

The cards: Use a pack of 51 cards, made by removing one queen from a regular pack.

To play: Deal all the cards out one at a time. Before play starts, each player shows and retires any pairs of like rank. After that, the player at the dealer's left takes one card, unseen, from the player at his left. If this makes a pair, it is also tabled, and the player continues. When the card taken does not make a pair, play passes on to the next player, who in turn takes a card from the next player. In this way, all cards eventually pair up except one queen, and the player holding it is declared "Old Maid."

Tip: After one pair of queens has been tabled, only body language can tell you who might have the remaining lone queen. Even so, it's hard to know which card that queen might be. Is the player in the diagram below encouraging you to take the card sticking out? Is that card safe? Unless you know, it's simply a matter of luck to avoid the Old Maid.

Variations: Instead of removing a queen, randomly remove from the pack one card that no one sees. In this way, only at the very end will all the players discover which card in actuality was the Old Maid.

For a quicker game, you can shrink the pack by omitting all cards of several ranks.

Draw cards from your neighbor's hand, seeing the card backs only.

PANGUINGUE

Panguingue, or Pan, is a gambling game especially popular out West that is also an enjoyable party game. It grew out of Coon Can and uses the same cards, only lots more of them! It also has a language of its own.

Number of players: up to 15, best when limited to eight

Objects: to meld certain groups of cards (conditions) and to be the first to go out (meld all cards)

The cards: Shuffle together five or more Coon Can packs (regular packs of 52 cards with all 8s, 9s, and 10s omitted). Aces are low.

To play: Unlike in other games, in Pan the deal and play rotate counterclockwise (to the right).

Deal ten cards to each player, in batches of five. Leave the remaining stock in the center of the table, turning its top card over to begin a discard pile.

Dropping: Each player decides whether to drop or play after looking at his or her hand. If you drop, throw in two chips. These chips will go to the winner of the hand. Dropping is also known as going on top, because the forfeited cards are stacked on the foot of the stock. The discards don't belong to the stock; you cannot play them.

If you decide to play, you must stay in the game until the end. The closest remaining player to the dealer's right goes first. The object of play is to meld 11 cards. A meld must consist of at least three cards in a group or sequence. A group is three or more cards of the same rank; a sequence is any three cards of the same suit, in sequence.

At each turn, you may take the upcard if you can meld it or add it on to a meld you already have. Otherwise, draw the top card of the stock. After drawing, table any melds you may have, and discard one card.

There are two types of melds: payoff melds (conditions) and nonpayoff melds. When you lay down a condition, each active player immediately pays you according to the chart below. Note that spades score double in all conditions.

All 3s, 5s, and 7s are valle cards, meaning they are cards that have value. Cards of any other rank (square cards) do not have value.

Any group of valle cards, different suits	1 chip
Any group of valle cards, same suit	2 chips
	(4 chips in spades)
Any group of nonvalle cards, same suit	1 chip
	(2 chips in spades)
Any sequence of A-2-3	1 chip
	(2 chips in spades)
Any sequence of J-Q-K	1 chip
	(2 chips in spades)

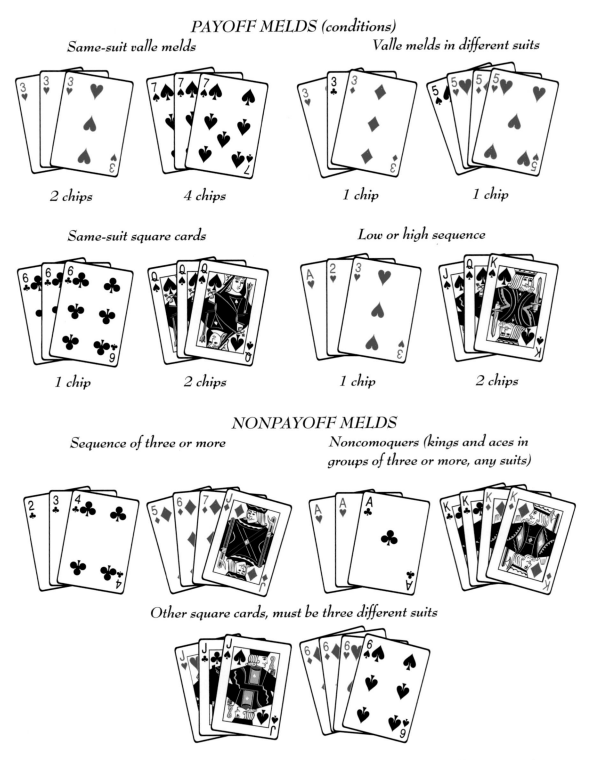

PAYOFF MELDS (conditions)

Same-suit valle melds · Valle melds in different suits

2 chips · 4 chips · 1 chip · 1 chip

Same-suit square cards · Low or high sequence

1 chip · 2 chips · 1 chip · 2 chips

NONPAYOFF MELDS

Sequence of three or more · Noncomoquers (kings and aces in groups of three or more, any suits)

Other square cards, must be three different suits

Groups of three or more square cards must be three different suits. With three different suits, however, you can lay off any duplicates at that time as well.

Sequences must be either low or high; for example, ♥K-♥A-♥2 is not a valid meld. ♣5-♦6-♠7 is not a valid meld either, because a sequence must be all of the same suit.

Laying off cards: You may lay off cards onto your own melds, but not onto other players' melds. Whenever you lay off an additional card on a pay spread, each player pays you again. *Exception:* Payment for extending a same-suit valle card spread pays half—just 1 chip, and 2 in spades.

Switching: You can rearrange or switch your own melds in two ways: You can take the fourth of a group and use it in another meld, and you can reshape sequence melds.

> ### Special Terms in Pan
>
> **Condition:** a spread that pays to its owner
>
> **Going on top:** dropping out before play starts
>
> **Noncomoquers:** all kings and aces
>
> **Rope:** a sequential meld
>
> **Spread:** any meld
>
> **Square cards:** As, 2s, 4s, 6s, Js, Qs, Ks
>
> **Valle cards:** 3s, 5s, 7s

Tips: The most important decision is whether to play a hand or pay the penalty and go on top. Usually you should stay in a hand if it contains

By taking the ♥6 (the fourth card from the meld) and adding it to the ♥5 and ♥7 from your hand, you form a rope.

Here, the cards have been rearranged to form a condition in spades! Collect 2 chips from every player.

Forcing: If at your turn the top discard can be laid off onto your melds, you are not obliged to take it unless another player demands that you do. This is called forcing. Upon adding the card to your meld, you must then discard.

Scoring: Whoever goes out first is the winner. Winner receives 1 chip from every player who did not drop, plus additional payment for all his or her conditions. In effect, then, the winner is paid twice for his or her payoff melds.

valle cards and others that may give you pay spreads. You should also stay in the game if your hand offers good possibilities of melding.

Variations: Panguingue houses often use eight Coon Can packs, omitting one suit of spades, leaving 310 cards. Sometimes an extra ♠3, ♠5, ♠7, ♠2, and ♠Q are also removed. In such games, the player with the lowest card receives the first deal, and thereafter the winner of each deal receives cards first.

PIQUET

Piquet is over 550 years old! Legend says it was invented by a knight who fought with Joan of Arc. In 1743, Piquet was one of five games covered in a treatise on games. Packed with French verbiage, Piquet has flourished in England, where it's pronounced "picket."

Number of players: two

Object: to outscore your opponent over six deals (a partie)

The cards: Use a pack of 32 cards. (Remove all 2s through 6s from a standard pack.) Aces are high.

To play: Deal 12 cards to each player and place the remaining eight cards facedown in a talon.

The nondealer may then choose to discard at least one and not more than five cards in exchange for an equal number of cards from the top of the talon. If the nondealer exchanges fewer than five cards, the nondealer may peek at those he or she did not take. The dealer may then exchange for as many cards as the nondealer has left behind. The goal of both players in this exchange is to form scoring combinations (see "Declaring").

Carte blanche: When you're dealt no picture cards, you have carte blanche. Before the exchange, show your hand to your opponent and score 10 points.

Declaring: After the card exchanges, the players determine who has the better scoring combinations in three categories: point, sequence, and sets, in that order.

Point. The suit with the highest point count (aces count 11, face cards 10, and other cards their face value) wins 1 point for each card. For example, the dealer's ♠A-♠Q-♠J-♠10-♠8

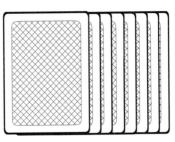

The nondealer discards ♠7, ♦9, and ♦8 and takes the top three talon cards. Since the nondealer discarded only three cards, he or she may peek at the next two talon cards and put them back in place.

Nondealer

Dealer

The dealer has a great-looking hand, but the nondealer's is even better. (The nondealer's hand is the same one as illustrated on page 42 after the three exchange cards: ♥Q-♥9-♠9.) The nondealer's point is a seven-card suit (♥A-♥K-♥Q-♥J-♥10-♥9-♥8) with a higher count than the dealer's (♣A-♣K-♣Q-♣10-♣9-♣8-♣7). The nondealer scores 7 for point. The nondealer's seven-card sequence is worth 17, and the three-card sequence (♠J-♠10-♠9) is worth 3: The nondealer scores 20 in sequences. The nondealer also has a group of four (♥J-♠J-♣J-♦J), which beats the dealer's trios (aces, kings): The nondealer scores 14 for this quatorze. The dealer, beaten in every category, does not score at all!

(49) beats the nondealer's ♦A-♦K-♦Q-♦9-♦8 (48), for a score of 5 (1 per card).

Sequence. The longest sequence in a single suit (minimum three cards) wins. If players have sequences of the same length, the one headed by the higher card wins. A sequence of three cards (a tierce) scores 3. A sequence of four (a quart) scores 4. A sequence of five or more scores the number of cards plus 10.

Sets. Sets are three or four cards of the same rank. A player with a foursome (a quatorze)—for instance, ♦Q-♥Q-♣Q-♠Q—beats a threesome (a trio)—♠A-♣A-♥A—regardless of rank; but in sets the same size, then the highest rank scores. Trios score 3 points and quatorzes score 14 points.

The nondealer begins the dialogue, starting with point. In the example given for "Point," the nondealer would say, "48," and the dealer would say, "Not good, 49." In each group only the

player with the winning meld scores. That player may also score for all other qualifying melds in that category. If players tie for best in a category, neither scores. For strategic reasons, you may choose not to declare a meld. This is called sinking the meld.

The play: Play to 12 tricks with no trump suits. The nondealer leads any card to the first trick. The highest card of the suit led wins the trick, and the winner of a trick plays to the next. In the play, score 1 point for every trick you lead, and 1 for every trick opponent leads that you win. For example, if the nondealer wins the first two tricks but loses the third, the nondealer has still scored the first 3 points of play, which can be significant in the scoring. The winner of the last trick scores 1 bonus point. Whoever wins more tricks scores a 10-point bonus, but if one player wins all 12 tricks, called a capot, the bonus is 40 points. Thus, if you lead and win all 12 tricks, you score 53 (12 for the leads, 1 for last trick, and 40 for capot).

In the illustrated hand on page 43, the nondealer would likely take the first seven tricks and score 8 points (1 point per lead). The dealer would take the last five tricks and score 6 points, including 1 for last trick.

Scoring: If you score the first 30 (or more) points of a hand, you score either the pique or repique bonus.

Pique bonus (30 points). If the nondealer scores the first 30 points in card combinations and trick-taking, the nondealer earns a 30-point bonus for pique. The dealer cannot win pique, because the nondealer automatically scores 1 for leading.

Repique bonus (60 points). If either player scores 30 or more points just in card combinations before opponent scores any, that player wins the 60-point repique bonus. In the hand shown on page 43, the nondealer scores the first 41 points in card melds, earning 60 points more for repique.

By custom, players announce their running totals throughout the hand, writing scores down at the end. Deal alternates, with six deals constituting a Piquet partie, or game. At the end of the partie, if both players have more than 100 points, the winner gets the difference in scores, plus a 100-point game bonus. However, if the loser has under 100 points, the winner, regardless of score, gets both scores combined, as well as the 100-point game bonus. The loser is said to be rubiconned, having not crossed the rubicon of 100 points.

Tip: In play, much depends on who leads first. Take a look at the hand shown on page 43. Switch the players' seats and the dealer would take every trick, if only the dealer could go first!

This rule affects your card-exchanging strategy. The dealer may need to keep strength in each suit to avoid giving up a capot. On the other hand, the nondealer can discard all cards of a suit, to increase the chance of a capot.

Variation: Instead of playing a Piquet partie with six deals, play *Piquet au Cent,* in which the game ends as soon as one player reaches 100 points.

POKER

Poker has endless variants, but they fall into three main groups: Draw Poker, Stud Poker, and Hold 'Em Poker. The standard poker game rewards the best (highest) hand, but there are numerous forms of Lowball Poker where the worst hand wins. In recent years, there's been a surge of High-Low Poker, where the best hand and the worst hand get to divide the same pot.

General Poker rules
- Each player receives a stack or stacks of chips.
- Deal and betting proceed clockwise (to the left).
- At the showdown (end of the hand), the last to bet—or to raise the bet—shows first.
- Players calling the final bet have a right to see the cards of all others who call.
- If at any point only one player is left, that hand wins and need not be shown.

Rank of hands in Poker
Royal flush: five sequential cards of the same suit to the ace (♥10-♥J-♥Q-♥K-♥A)
Straight flush: any five sequential cards of the same suit (♥7-♥8-♥9-♥10-♥J)
Four of a kind: all four cards of a rank (♣6-♥6-♦6-♠6)

Full house: three of a kind plus a pair (♥3-♠3-♣3-♦10-♠10)
Flush: any five cards of a suit (♠Q-♠9-♠8-♠5-♠2)
Straight: five cards in sequence, any suits; aces high or low (♦A-♥2-♣3-♦4-♠5)
Three of a kind: three cards of one rank, the rest unmatched (♠K-♦K-♥K-♣9-♦7)
Two pair: two different pairs of two cards of a rank, the rest unmatched (♦J-♣J-♥8-♣8-♥5)
One pair: two cards of a rank, the rest unmatched (♦J-♣J-♥8-♣7-♥5)
High card: no combination; aces high (♣A-♠7-♥9-♣10-♣4)

Between hands of the same type, the higher-ranked hand wins. For example, a flush headed by a jack (♣J-♣9-♣5-♣3-♣2) beats a flush to the 10 (♦10-♦9-♦8-♦5-♦3); queens up (♥Q-♦Q-♣3-♠3-♥4) beats 9s up (♠9-♥9-♣8-♥8-♠K).

Wild cards: In some games, the dealer may call certain cards wild—that is, they can stand for any other card. Sometimes a joker is added as a wild card. Deuces wild (all four of them) is another popular choice. Another favorite is One-eyes wild (the three face cards in profile: ♦K, ♥J, and ♠J).

Lowball Poker: Lowball Poker can be played in as many styles as High Only Poker. There is usually a round of betting, a draw, then another betting round, and a showdown. Aces rank low. The hand that ranks as the poorest poker hand wins. For example, ♠7-♣3-♥9-♦4-♣5 (a 9-low) beats ♥4-♣A-♦2-♠J-♥3 (a jack-low).

Most lowball versions disregard flushes and straights and pay attention only to the number value of the cards, so that 7-6-5-4-3 is a 7-low. (Make very sure that all players are clear on this.) When hands competing for low have the same worst cards, look to the next worst card. For example, 8-5-4-2-A beats 8-6-3-2-A.

High-Low Poker: In High-Low Poker, the best hand and the worst hand divide the pot. Any form of poker—Draw, Stud, or Hold 'Em—can be played High-Low.

The declaration: In most games, players declare, before the showdown, whether they are going high, low, or high and low. In some games, this is done out loud, by going around the table starting with the last raiser or bettor. This reduces some surprises and gives a certain positional advantage for which to play.

A more common practice is to declare silently but at the same time using chips or coins. At a signal, players either put no chips in their hand to go low, one chip in their hand to go high, or two chips to go high and low. In some games, this is the final action, after which the winners and losers are sorted out. In some games these declarations are followed by one more betting round (the drive) that gives bluffers and legitimate hands one more chance to raise the pot. Since one player may have a lock on half the pot, High-Low poker limits raises to three per round.

Most High-Low games encourage you to go for high and low on the same deal, if you've got the right hand. This is easy in seven-card games, where you can use different sets of cards for each direction you go. In five-card games, it must be clear whether a 2-3-4-5-6 straight can be low, that is, a 6-low. If you go high-low but lose in either direction (high or low), you're out of the hand.

General terms in Poker

Ante: an initial stake each player places in the pot

Betting in the blind: betting without seeing your cards

Bluffing: betting or raising with a weak hand

Broadway: a straight to the ace

Call: to equal a bet made by another player

Check: to pass

Drop: to quit a hand

Fold: to quit a hand

(the) Goods: a real hand, no bluff

Hole cards: in stud poker, facedown cards

Openers: a good enough card combination to meet a minimum requirement

Pat hand: a hand you don't draw to

Pot: all the bets in the center of the table

Pot limit: a dangerous game, where the bet limit is the sum of chips in the pot

Raise: to equal another player's bet and to add to it

Sandbag: to check (pass), and later raise in the same round

See a bet: to equal it, call

Sixth street: the last upcard in seven-card stud, before a downcard is dealt

Stand pat: to draw no cards

Trips: three of a kind

Wheel: a hand good for both high and low

DRAW POKER

Number of players: two to seven

Object: to win the pot, either by being the only player left or by having the best cards

The cards: Use a regular pack of 52 cards.

To play: Each player antes one chip. Cards are dealt one by one until each player has five. The first player then may bet or check, but once a player has bet, each player in turn either folds or sees the bet (and perhaps raises it).

Once all bets and raises are called, the dealer proceeds to ask each player in turn how many cards they wish to draw. The maximum number of cards a player can draw is three. Each player casts unwanted cards aside, and the dealer deals replacements. The dealer's own draw should be clearly announced, for example, the dealer may state, "Dealer takes two." A player who draws no cards is said to stand pat.

Once players receive all their new cards, the final round of betting takes place, beginning with the player who made the last raise or bet and continuing clockwise. Most games establish a betting limit, which on the second round is usually double the first.

When all bets and raises are called again, there is a showdown to see whose hand is best. Usually the last bettor shows first, and others may choose to fold their hands if beaten. However, the remaining players in the pot have a right to see all hands that called.

If all players pass on the first round, throw in the hand. The deal passes to the left, and another round of five cards is dealt. Leave the chips in the pot, as players add another ante.

HOLD 'EM POKER

Number of players: two to ten

Object: to join your two cards with any three on the table to make the best hand that wins the pot

The cards: Use a regular pack of 52 cards.

To play: After each player antes, deal two cards facedown to each player and five cards facedown to the center of the table. Starting with the player at the dealer's left, each player may check or bet. Once a player bets, subsequent players must fold unless they see (or raise) the bet.

Once all first-round bets are called, the dealer turns over the first three facedown cards. These are called the flop. You must use both your hole cards (the two cards dealt facedown) with three from the table to form the best possible hand.

Whoever was the last bettor starts a new round of betting, after which the dealer turns up one more card from the center of the table. Another betting round ensues, and then the dealer turns over the last card for a final betting round. Whoever has the best hand and is still in the betting wins the pot.

STUD POKER

Number of players: two to eight

Object: to win the pot, either by being the only player left or by having the best cards

The cards: Use a regular pack of 52 cards.

To play: In Five-Card Stud Poker, each player antes. Deal one card down and one up to each player.

The player with the highest card showing starts with a check or a bet, and betting continues clockwise around the table. As soon as there's a bet, the players following must, in turn, either fold or call (and perhaps raise) the bet.

Once all bets are called, the remaining players each receive another upcard. The player with the best hand showing starts another round of betting.

Each round of cards dealt up is followed by a betting round. The final round of bets occurs when all players left in the hand have four upcards. This round of betting should have a higher limit than the previous rounds. Also, if any player shows a pair at any time, the bet limit is raised.

After the final bets, the bettor—or last raiser—is usually first to turn over the hole card (the first card dealt facedown). If no one calls the last bet or raise, the winner gathers the pot and isn't obliged to show anyone the winning hand.

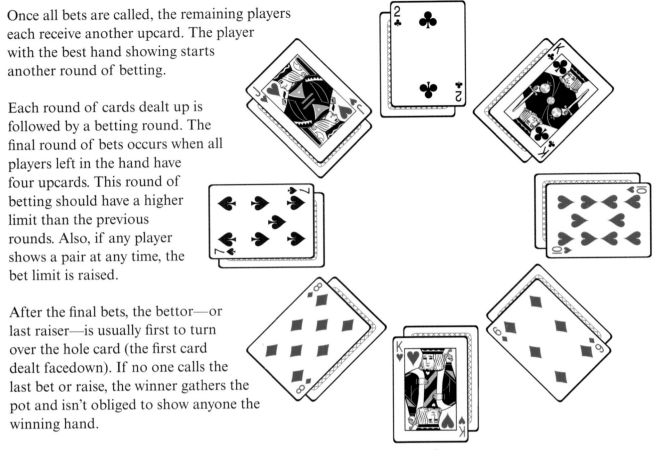

Dealer

The ♣K is the high card. This player may check or bet. If ♣K bets, then the player with the ♥10 sees the bet, or else drops (shown by turning the ♥10 over), and so on with each player around the table. Since the ♣K was dealt first, it has betting priority over the ♥K.

You and one player remain from the hand dealt above. You now show a pair of kings. Your opponent must have an ace in the hole to have any chance to win. If you have a king, 6, or 4 in the hole, you are a sure winner. Bet only as much as you think your opponent might call. If you are not a sure winner, however, you must decide what to do. In situations like this, a poker face is called for!

RUMMY

Rummy originated in the camps and saloons of the old West, where it was known as Whiskey Poker because it was played for drinks. As times changed, so did the game. It received many new names and traveled in many directions, leaving favorite versions all around. Every Rummy game has its own appeal.

Melds in all Rummy games: Melds in Rummy consist of groups of three or more cards of the same rank or sequences of three or more cards in one suit.

GIN RUMMY

Number of players: two or four (as partners)

Object: to meld your cards and score for Gin or Knock

The cards: Use a regular pack of 52 cards. Aces are low.

To play: Deal ten cards to each player. Turn one card up—the knock card—to begin a discard pile. Place the remaining cards facedown next to it as a draw pile, or talon.

The nondealer may take the knock card and discard. If the nondealer declines the knock card, the dealer may take it and discard. Should neither player want it, the nondealer draws the top card from stock and discards.

Turns alternate. At each play, take either the top discard or the top card from stock and then discard. Look to match cards in your hand into melds. When all your cards are melded, call, "Gin" (or "Gin Rummy"), discard facedown, and show your hand.

Knocking: If you wish to stop the round before you or your opponent reaches gin, you may knock. Simply discard facedown and say, "Knock." Or, simply rap the table, put down your melds, and set aside your unmatched cards—called deadwood. Your total deadwood

Sample melds in Rummy.

Groups of three or four cards of the same rank.

Sequences of three or more consecutive cards in one suit. Aces are low only.

count must not be greater than the original knock card (see "Scoring" for card values). If the knock card was ♦8 and you have ♣10-♣J-♣Q-♣K, ♠9-♣9-♥9, ♦A, ♠2, ♣4, your deadwood cards offer little melding hope. Since their count totals only 7, you should knock.

Laying off: After a player knocks, the opponent has the opportunity to lay off any possible melds onto the tabled melds. In this way, the opponent can reduce his or her point total (see "Scoring"). Laying off is not permitted after a gin.

Scoring: Unmelded picture cards count 10, and all others their face value (aces count 1). If you gin, score your opponent's deadwood total, plus a 25-point bonus. If you knock, score the difference between your knock-count and your opponent's remaining deadwood cards after making any layoffs.

As sometimes happens—especially after laying off—your knock count may be greater than your opponent's deadwood. In this case, your opponent scores the difference in count, if any, plus a 20-point bonus for the underknock (also called undercut). If your opponent lays off every unmelded card, the bonus is 25 points for ginning off.

The hand is thrown in if neither player makes gin or knocks. Common practice is to stop play

when two talon cards are still left. Game is generally played to 100 points.

Tips: Gin is a good game for memory-training: It pays to recall which cards have already been played, especially the ones your opponent takes. Be aware, however, that your opponent will also notice the discards you pick up!

A few helpful don'ts

• Don't pick up a discard unless it gives you a meld or unless you have a very poor hand and your pick opens up a few chances. An exception might be to pick up a low-count discard (an ace or deuce) when you have a bad hand and a safe discard to make.

• Don't hold on to a high melding chance that only one card can fill. For instance, don't hold on to ♦10-♦Q if you can draw any better or lower cards.

• Don't expect to find a third ace when you have two, unless you get lucky and draw it from the draw pile. That's not a card your opponent would discard except with a very good hand.

• Don't play for gin when you have the opportunity to knock early.

Variation: In *Three-Handed Gin Rummy,* one player sits out while the other two play a hand. The player sitting out takes the place of the player with the losing hand. Each player keeps score separately.

KNOCK RUMMY

Number of players: two to six

Object: to knock when you have a lower deadwood count than any of your opponents

The cards: Use a regular pack of 52 cards. Aces are low.

To play: For two players, deal ten cards each. For three or four players, deal seven cards each. With five or six players, deal just six cards each, leaving enough cards for each player to have several turns.

Knock Rummy proceeds like Gin Rummy, with two major differences. The first difference is that you may knock on any turn, with any deadwood count, and the second is that no cards are laid off on the knocker's melds.

As the play rotates, the discard is available only to the player whose turn it currently is.

Scoring: When someone knocks, show your cards, separating melded combinations from deadwood. Whoever has the lowest deadwood count wins the difference from each other player. If you knock and are tied, the player you tie with is deemed the winner and collects from the others. When you knock and do not have the lowest hand, pay an extra 10 points to the winner of the hand.

When you knock with a fully melded hand (going rummy), you win a 25-point bonus from each player, plus their deadwood counts.

Tips: With two players, if you're dealt a deadwood count in the 40s, that may often be

lower than your opponent's count. Since losing costs an additional 10-point penalty, you should probably make a quick knock only if under 35.

With more players, the added bonus for going rummy may influence you to play out a hand with an early meld. That's okay if your deadwood cards are relatively high (7s and above) or if your unmelded cards have a good chance of making a meld. But if your deadwood count is low, you should end the round as early as possible—before your opponents draw enough lucky cards to win.

OLD-FASHIONED RUMMY (STRAIGHT RUMMY)

Number of players: two to six

Object: to get rid of all your cards by melding and by laying cards off onto others' melds

The cards: Use a regular pack of 52 cards. Aces are low.

To play: For two, three, or four players, deal six or seven cards each. For five or six players, deal six cards each.

Turn one card up to begin the discard pile. Starting with the player at the dealer's left, either take the top discard or draw the top card from the stock. Before discarding, you may table melds or lay off cards on other melds.

The game ends when someone has melded or laid off every card from their hand. A final discard is not required. If no one can go out, and you've gone through the discard pile a second time, throw in the hand.

Scoring: Each hand is scored independently. Winner scores for all cards still held in players' hands, whether in melds or not. If you go rummy—go out on one play—you win double.

500 RUMMY

Number of players: two to eight (Three to five players work best.)

Object: to score points for melds and to meld all your cards

The cards: For two to four players, use a regular pack of 52 cards. For five or more players, use two packs of 52 cards. Aces are high or low.

To play: For two players, deal ten cards to each player; for three to eight players, deal seven cards to each player.

Melds score according to the cards they contain: High aces count 15; low aces 1; face cards 10; all others their face value.

In other Rummy games, the discard pile is a tight stack, with only its top card in view. Here, the discard pile is spread out so that all cards are in view.

Play starts at the dealer's left, and at your turn you may take the top card from stock, or you can take any card in the discard pile—not just the top discard—as long as you use it as part of a meld. You also have to take all cards above the discard you take. Usually this is helpful, since your goal is to meld many points.

Besides making melds, you can also lay cards off on your own or others' melds. Since you tally your melds at the end of the hand, keep layoffs on others' melds within your own melding area.

The game ends when any player goes out—melds or lays off every card, with or without a final discard. No further melds, plays, or discards may occur. If no player should go out, the game ends when the entire stock is exhausted.

Scoring: At the end of play, total your melded cards, then subtract the count of cards left in your hand (whether meldable or not). Record each player's score. There is no added bonus for going out.

Tips: The strategy of 500 Rummy is nearly the opposite of other Rummy games. You should keep high cards longer, because they're worth more. Since a discard can be available later, you may break up a low-scoring meld, allowing you to pick up more cards later. However, be careful when doing this, because someone else may have the same idea, and you could lose your card!

Players keep cards laid off on sequence melds nearby, for scoring later. In this case, the ♣5 and ♣6 have been laid off on another player's ♣2-♣3-♣4 sequence.

SCHAFKOPF

Also spelled Schafskopf, this forerunner of Skat emphasizes skill in taking tricks. In the United States, it's often known by its translated name, Sheepshead.

Number of players: three (Four or five players may sit at the table, with players taking turns sitting out.)

Object: to win at least 61 of 120 points available in tricks

The cards: Use a 32-card pack (omit all 2s through 6s from a standard pack). All queens, jacks, and diamonds are trump cards. The plain suits—spades, clubs, and hearts—rank A (high)-10-K-9-8-7.

To play: The three players are called forehand (to the dealer's left), middlehand, and endhand. Deal one round of three cards each, then two facedown cards—called the skat—that are set aside, a round of four cards, and another round of three cards, for a total of ten cards per player.

Determine who will be the Player against the two others. Starting with forehand, pick up the skat and then discard two cards to accept the role of Player. If forehand doesn't accept, the option moves to the middlehand and so on. If no one accepts, play the deal as a Least (see "Scoring").

No matter who is the Player, forehand starts play by leading any card to the first trick. Always follow suit when able, but otherwise play any card. A trick is won by the highest trump card in it, or, lacking any trump cards, by the highest card of the suit led. Whoever wins a trick leads to the next until all ten tricks are taken.

Cards count as follows:

Ace	11 points
Ten	10 points
King	4 points
Queen	3 points
Jack	2 points
7, 8, and 9	0 points

Ranking in order from left to right, these are Schafkopf's permanent trump cards.

This hand represents an excellent take. You've got quite a few high trump cards, though you're missing the highest one. You haven't seen the skat yet, but you can plan already on exchanging the ♣ 10, which will count in your tricks later. When you get the chance to trump a plain suit, use the ♦ 10 to be sure of winning it.

At the end of play, each side counts points taken in tricks. The Player must win at least 61 of the 120 points in play (including the two discards in the count). The Player's two opponents work together to win points and defeat the Player. Their chief strategy is to smear each other's tricks with high-scoring cards.

Scoring: Each player gains or loses game points according to the following chart.

Points in play	Game points
61–90	2
91+ (Schneider)	4
winning all tricks (Schwarz)	6
31–60	–2
0–30	–4
winning no tricks	–6

When the hand is played at Least, everyone tries to take as few points as possible. Whoever has the lowest total wins 2 game points, and a player taking no tricks scores 4 game points. If two players tie for Least, whoever did not take the most recent trick (between the two) wins the 2 game points. If all three players tie at 40 points each, endhand scores the 2 game points. If you

take all the tricks, you lose 4 game points. Play to 10 game points.

Tips: To help you remember the rank of queens and jacks as trump, remember the word CaSHeD—Clubs, Spades, Hearts, Diamonds.

To accept the role of Player, you almost certainly need more than your one-third share of the 14 trump cards. But since you'll need to score points, it helps to have an ace or two.

Of the 120 points, 75 come from the aces, 10s, and kings of the plain suits, which have only six cards each. You can't count on everyone following even to the first lead. In fact, the Player's two discards very often create a void in at least one plain suit. As a defender, you may find that the way to win an ace is to be able to play it when your codefender is winning a trick in another suit. Especially when you have very few trump cards, look for chances to smear—to discard an ace or 10—on your side's trick.

Variation: In some games, a Least is played with no suit as trump, with each suit ranked, from high to low, A-K-Q-J-10-9-8-7.

SETBACK

Setback is a quick game of trump, filled with strategy and surprise. Also known as Pitch and Auction Pitch, it is a descendant of the Mississippi riverboat game Seven Up.

Number of players: three to five (However, two to seven may play.)

Object: to score points by winning high trump, low trump, jack of trump, and game

The cards: Use a regular pack of 52 cards. Aces are high.

To play: Deal six cards to each player, in bunches of three. Starting at the dealer's left, players each have one chance to pass or bid. A bid is a number—one through four—and must be a higher number than any earlier bid.

The high bidder (the pitcher) plays against everybody else. Four possible points can be won in play: high (the highest trump in play), low (the lowest trump in play), jack (the jack of trump, not always in play), and game (the highest total of cards won in play). Aces count 4; kings 3; queens 2; jacks 1; and 10s 10.

The pitcher always leads a card to begin play. The suit led becomes trump. Because of this rule, you can silently bid four (the highest bid) by pitching a card to indicate your trump lead.

Always follow suit when possible. If unable to follow suit, play any card. Each trick is won by the highest trump card it contains or, if it contains no trump, by the highest card of the suit led.

Although the defenders work together to set back the pitcher, they keep separate piles of the tricks they've each taken, since each independently scores any points earned.

In a four-player game, you win the bid at two. You need to make any 2 of the 4 points. Here, low and game are the most likely points you'll win. Careful play should clear out your opponents' trump cards, leaving an open path for your ♣2 to score the low point and for you to win another trick with the ♦ 10.

Scoring: If you make your bid, you score all the points you won. If you don't make your bid, you lose—or are set back—the number you bid. Regardless of how the pitcher fared, defenders score their individually won points.

Whoever reaches 7 points wins the game. When two players are near 7, always tally high point first, followed by low, jack, and game.

SOLO

This popular trick-taking game—a cousin of Whist—gives players a chance to form occasional temporary partnerships. Since you don't ever have to change seats in this informal game, Solo is well suited to a long trip.

Number of players: four

Object: to win enough tricks to fulfill your contract

The cards: Use a regular pack of 52 cards. Aces are high.

To play: The turn to deal passes clockwise from the dealer. Deal 13 cards to each player, turning the dealer's last card up to specify a trump suit. The player at the dealer's left, eldest hand, acts first. Eldest hand may pass or make one of the calls in the following list. Calls are listed in rank from low to high.

Proposal (Prop): to take eight of 13 tricks with another player as a partner
Solo: to take five of 13 tricks playing alone against the three other players
Misère (me-ZAIR): to take no tricks, playing alone with no suit as trump
Abondance (Abundance): to take nine of 13 tricks, playing alone against three opponents, with a suit other than the upcard as trump

(When this is the final call, announce the trump suit before the opening lead is made.)
Misère Ouverte (me-ZAIR oo-VAIRT): to take no tricks, with no suit as trump, and with the hand exposed on the table (also called Spread)
Abondance in Trump (Royal Abondance): to take nine of 13 tricks, with the upcard suit as trump
Abondance Declared: to take all 13 tricks against the other players, naming a suit as trump

You may only make a call if it outranks a prior call. For example, if a player calls Misère, you cannot then call Prop or Solo.

Prop and Cop: A player proposes by saying, "I propose," or simply "Prop." Any player who has not passed may accept (Cop) the proposal, as long as a higher call has not been made. If you Prop and no one accepts, you may convert your call into a higher one or else throw in the hand.

A player who passes cannot later make a call, except eldest player, who may accept a proposal after passing.

Regardless of who makes the final call, eldest hand leads to the first trick. One exception is at Abondance Declared, when the caller leads first. The dealer should remember to pick up the upcard before the second trick.

Players follow suit whenever possible but otherwise may play any card. A trick is won by the highest trump card it contains or by the highest card of the suit led when it contains no trump. The winner of each trick leads to the next.

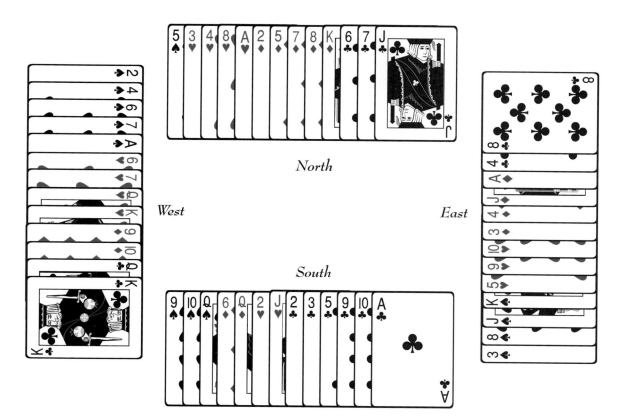

North

West

East

South

A typical Solo hand illustrating Prop and Cop. Hearts are turned as trump and West proposes with a good hand if joined by the right partner. North accepts on a hand without many high cards, but which will assist at hearts. East and South pass. West and North become partners for the hand. They will probably take nine or ten tricks together. West may start with the ♠A and then lead another spade, which North will trump. This is a good beginning, as the partners are using their trump cards one by one.

Scoring: Each deal of Solo is scored independently. You may collect, or pay off, according to this typical scoring scale:

Prop and Cop	5 points
Solo	10 points
Misère	20 points
Abondance	30 points
Misère Ouverte	30 points
Abondance in Trump	40 points
Abondance Declared	60 points

Tips: Hands scoring more than Misère don't come up often, but they are recognizable. An Abondance hand might be ♣A-♣K-♣J-♣10-♣9-♣6-♦A-♦K-♦10-♦5-♦4-♠5-♥7. A Misère Ouverte could be ♣A-♣10-♣6-♣5-♣3-♣2-♦J-♦7-♦4-♦3-♦2-♠4-♥3.

Most Solo hands revolve around contracts of Prop and Cop. As the illustrated deal shows, you can take tricks with low cards if your side has the majority of trump cards. In that deal, North seized the opportunity to Cop. Had North passed, East might have accepted West's Prop, but this would be a closer battle for eight tricks.

Note that for Misère, you can't have any flaw: In the hand shown, North can be forced to win a heart trick or a club trick; South could be made to win a spade or a diamond at a Misère bid.

SPADES

It's curious that not much has been written about this widely known, easy-to-learn trick-taking game. It's gathering new devotees from within urban America, on college campuses, and even in cyberspace!

Number of players: four, playing as partners

Object: to win the number of tricks bid by you and your partner

The cards: Use a regular pack of 52 cards. Aces are high.

To play: Partners sit opposite each other. The dealer deals 13 cards to each player. Spades are always the trump suit. There's one round of bidding, which starts at the dealer's left. The first two players both bid the number of tricks—or books—they expect to take, while the second player in each partnership bids the total for the pair. For example, you deal, the player on your left bids four, your partner bids three, the next player bids five, and you bid seven. Your side has bid for seven tricks, your opponents have bid for five tricks.

The following are several special bids that are optional in Spades.

10 for Two: a contract for ten books without a partner, with a two-to-one payoff

Nil: a bid by the first bidder for a side for no tricks, which the partner must convert to four tricks

Blind Nil: similar to Nil except the player may not look at the cards beforehand (Before play you and your partner may exchange one card. Your side must be down by 200 points to go for a bid of Blind Nil.)

When you are dealt many spades and a pretty good hand, you might try 10 for Two on your own. Save bids such as seven and eight for hands that need your partner's help to reach ten books.

The player at the dealer's left may lead any card other than a spade to the first trick. You must follow suit if able, otherwise you may play any card. The highest spade played or, if no spade was played, the highest card of the suit led wins the trick.

The winner of each trick leads to the next. Until a spade is played on a nonspade lead, you can't lead spades unless all you have in your hand are spades. When you win a book, gather it in a packet that everyone can count with your other books.

Scoring: If your side makes its bid, score the bid number times 10, plus 1 for each extra trick, called a sandbag. If your side fails to make at least the amount bid, you lose ten times the number of tricks bid. For example, your side bids seven, and your opponents bid five. You make nine tricks, while your opponents make four. Your side scores 72 points (7×10, plus two sandbags); opponents lose 50 (5×10).

If you succeed at 10 for Two, you win 200 points, but if you fail, you lose 100. For Nil, you win 100 or lose 100 as the case may be, but for Blind Nil you win 200 at the risk of 100.

Sandbags: When your sandbags total ten, subtract 100 points from your score (don't add 10). This works as a slow penalty for underbidding the number of books you take. Any leftover sandbags start a new count to ten.

Play until one side reaches 500 points, or any agreed upon count.

Tips: Because of sandbags, winning extra books is no help, so be on the lookout for a situation where you have both the high card and the low card in a suit and can control winning a book or losing it. If you have ♠10-♠7, for example, and you know that the only spade remaining is an opponent's ♠8, depending upon the number of tricks you want, you can choose whether to win the ♠8 or lose it.

Variations: In some games, the ♦2 is used as an extra trump card, ranking between the ace and king. Some games add a joker for an extra trump card and leave out a plain-suit deuce.

An interesting alternative to start the hand is for all players to put out their lowest club (or lowest diamond, lacking clubs) for the first book. The high club in this book wins it and leads to the next trick. With the first book played this way, the strategies for bidding and play are different.

Some Spades games allow a generous amount of informal chat between partners before deciding on their bid. You can say nearly anything except what cards you hold.

SPITE AND MALICE

Related to Russian Bank, this game has an ebb and flow, a give and take, and many shifts of pace. Because you can often regulate how much to do on one turn, you can make plays that annoy and frustrate your opponent. It has become a curious favorite of married couples.

Number of players: two

Object: to be the first player to get rid of all cards from your payoff pile

The cards: Use two packs of 52 cards, plus their four jokers. Aces are low. A joker can stand for any card except an ace.

To play: Players sit across from each other with a large playing area between them. Shuffle all four jokers with one of the decks to create a shared draw pile. Place it facedown between the two players. Shuffle and deal out the other deck card by card, giving each player a facedown 26-card payoff pile.

Players each turn up their top payoff card, leaving it faceup on the pile. Whoever shows the lower card deals a five-card hand from the draw pile to each player. The nondealer plays first, turns alternating thereafter.

At each turn you are required to play any aces you have in your hand or on your payoff pile into the middle of the table. An ace begins a center stack that is built card by card up to king. Suit and color don't matter. Each available deuce is also required to be played onto a center stack whenever possible. If there is no ace in the center, you must wait to play the 2.

In addition, you may choose to make any, all, or none of the other possible plays available:

- You can play one card from your hand to begin one of your four side stacks (start only one side stack per turn, until you have four). These side stacks give you a chance to organize your discards.
- You can play one or more cards from your hand onto one or more of your side stacks. Each card you add to a side stack, however, must be either the same rank as the topmost card showing or one rank below it (any 9 on any 10, for instance). Each player can play only to his or her own side stacks and only with cards from his or her hand. Color and suit don't matter.
- You can move the topmost card from one side stack either onto another side stack or to start a brand-new side stack (unless you already have four side stacks).
- You can play a card from your hand, your payoff pile, or your side stacks onto the center stacks. Play a 2 on an ace, a 3 on a 2, and so on upward to king. Suit and color don't matter.

Before beginning each turn, take cards from the draw pile to bring your hand back to five cards, replacing any cards you played on your last turn.

Keep playing until you can't or choose not to make any further move. Just say, "That's it," and your opponent takes his or her turn.

When a center stack is built up to the king, shuffle the cards from that stack back into the draw pile. You can wait for a few stacks to accumulate.

Bonus turns: Whenever you play all five cards from your hand in one turn, you get an extra turn. Take five new cards from the draw pile and keep playing.

When neither player can—or will—make a play, the game is blocked. In a blocked game you must make any obvious plays your opponent requests in order to keep the game moving.

Scoring: If you play out your entire payoff pile, you win a point for each card remaining in your opponent's payoff pile, plus a 10-point bonus. In a blocked game, whoever has fewer payoff-pile cards left scores the difference, with no bonus. Play to 25 points, or to any other agreed upon number.

Tips: Your immediate goal is always to reduce your payoff pile, so it is usually worth spending a joker or two—if need be—to play off your current payoff card. The next card you turn up may be easy to play off.

A constant goal is to make play difficult for your opponent. For instance, try to build center stacks just past the rank of opponent's current payoff-pile card.

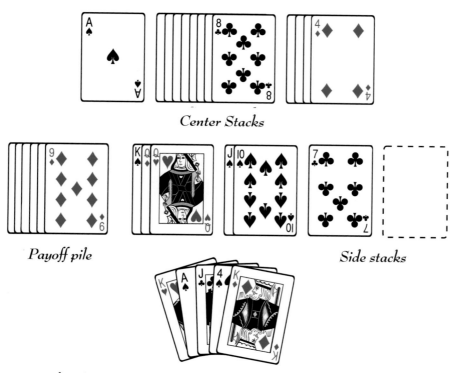

Center Stacks

Payoff pile

Side stacks

It's your turn. You must play ♠A to start a new center stack. You should also play ♦9 from your payoff pile on top of the ♣8 in the center, and follow with the ♠10, ♣J from your hand, then ♥Q-♥K. You may also begin your fourth side stack with ♦K. Since you have a new payoff card to turn up, you may still have plays left this turn.

TWENTY-ONE

Don't confuse this game with the casino game of Blackjack, also called 21. Even children can play this easy-to-learn numbers game, and anyone can win! It also offers a chance to practice counting skills.

Number of players: two to seven

Object: to win as many cards as possible, without going over 21

The cards: Use a regular pack of 52 cards. Aces and picture cards count 1 point each, all others count their face value.

To play: Deal the cards out equally, and set aside any remaining cards. Starting at the dealer's left and continuing in a clockwise fashion, players build a card count up to 21. As each card is played, the new total is announced.

When you play a card that reaches 21 exactly, collect the cards in the center. However, when any card you have would go over 21, say, "Stop." The player on your right collects the cards. The player who said "Stop," begins the next count toward 21.

The hand is over when the final player gathers in the last cards.

Scoring: Players count the cards they've won, and each player's score is recorded. The first player to 50 points (or any other agreed upon total) wins.

A similar game called *Twenty-Nine* is intended for four players as partners. Deal 13 cards each. The player at the dealer's left begins by playing any card, and players follow in turn, stating the new total with each card played. If you can't play without going past 29, you must pass. Whoever reaches 29 exactly wins the trick. The next player then begins a new count. Eight tricks are possible, although not always taken in play. The side with the most cards when no one can play to 29 exactly wins.

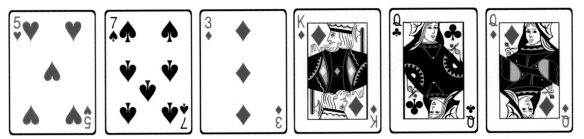

The count has gone 5-12-15-16-17-18. If you have a 3, you can score 21 exactly and win the cards. If you have an ace, deuce, or picture card, you can still play. Otherwise, say, "Stop." The player on your right gathers in the cards, and you begin a new count.

WAR

Along with Old Maid, War is one of the first card games we played as children. In practical terms, it rarely ends with a thorough defeat.

Number of players: two or more

Object: to win all the cards

The cards: Use a regular pack of 52 cards. Aces are high.

To play: Divide the pack equally into a facedown pile for each player. At about the same time, each player turns over their top card. Whoever has the higher card wins both cards, and the process is repeated. Place the cards you win on the bottom of your pile.

Occasionally, both players turn up cards of the same rank. This starts a war, in which each player lays off three more cards facedown and then turns up the next card. Whoever's card is higher wins all the cards from that war. If the cards are still tied, turn three more cards facedown and then turn the next card up to determine the winner.

The game ends when one player takes all the cards. You can try a shorter game, where you go through the cards just once or twice, and then see who has the most cards.

Variation: For three or more players, deal the cards out as equally as possible. Turn cards as before, and when players tie for best card, each plays two more facedown cards, with the next card turned up to decide a winner. Players not in the war must also contribute their next three cards. Play continues until one player has all the cards.

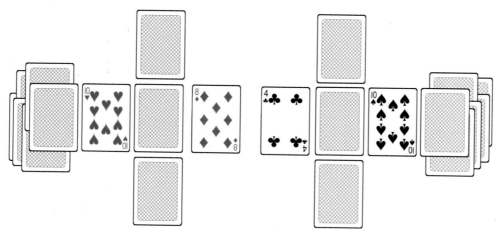

When there is a tie for a high card, a war is waged to determine the winner. Here, players were tied at 10, and the player with the ♦ 8 is the winner of this war.

GLOSSARY

Bid: a spoken declaration to win a certain number of tricks or points; also, to make such a declaration

Big Casino: in Casino, the ♦ 10

Build: in Casino, to combine two or more cards so they can be taken with another card; also, the combination itself

Canasta: natural canasta—a meld of seven cards of the same rank; mixed canasta—one to three cards replaced by wild cards

Contract: an agreement to win a certain number of tricks or points in a game or round

Crib: in Cribbage, the extra hand, formed by the players' discards and belonging to the dealer

Cutthroat: each player playing on his or her own

Deadwood: in Rummy games, cards in a player's hand that remain unmelded

Deal: to give out cards before play

Declaration: a statement to fulfill a contract

Deuce: a card of the rank of 2

Dix: in Pinochle, the 9 of trump

Draw: to take a new card or cards

Draw trump: to lead high trump in order to deplete opponent's hand of trump cards

Face card: a king, queen, or jack

Face value: the numerical value of a card

Flush: a set of cards all of the same suit

Follow suit: to play a card of the suit led

Game: a total number of points to achieve; also, what constitutes winning or ending a game

Gin: in Gin and Rummy games, a hand completely matched in melding sets, with no deadwood

Going out: playing, melding, or discarding final card

Hand: the cards a player holds; also, a deal of play

Kitty: a common chip-pool; also (in a few games) cards available for exchange

Knock: in Gin and Rummy games, to end play by laying down a hand that is not completely matched

Lay off: to play one or more cards according to allowable plays

Lead: to play the first card to a trick

Left bower: in Euchre, the jack of the same color as the trump suit

Little Casino: in Casino, the ♠ 2

Marriage: a king and queen of the same suit

Match: to equate by being of the same rank (or by another criterion)

Meld: a combination of cards with scoring value, generally three or more cards in sequence in one suit or all of the same rank; also, to show or play such a combination

No trump: the condition when no suit is trump in a trick-taking game

Pass: a spoken declaration not to make a bid; in Hearts, three hidden cards exchanged among the players

Peg: in Cribbage, to score points

Plain card: any 10, 9, 8, 7, 6, 5, 4, 3, 2, or ace

Pot: a pile of chips or counters collected by the winner

Right bower: in Euchre, the jack of the trump suit

Sequence: two or more cards in consecutive order

Skunk: in Cribbage, to win by at least 30 points, or 60 in a game of 121

Stock: the undealt cards available for future use

Table: the playing area; also, to lay down a meld on the playing area

Talon: portion of the pack reserved for later use during the deal

Trail: in Casino, to play a card to the table without building on or taking in other cards

Trey: card of the rank of 3

Trick: round of cards played, one by each player in turn

Trump: a suit of cards designated to be higher-ranking than any other suit; also, to play a trump card on a trick

Upcard: the first card turned up after a deal, often to begin play or initiate a discard pile

Void: a lack of a suit in a player's hand

Wild card: a card that can be designated by the holder to stand for any other card